HAVE A
LOVE
AFFAIR

WITH YOUR

HUSBAND

(Before Someone Else Does)

HAVE A LOVE AFFAIR

AFFAIR

WITH YOUR

HUSBAND

(Before Someone Else Does)

SUSAN KOHL AND
ALICE MILLER BREGMAN

ST. MARTIN'S PRESS
New York

HAVE A LOVE AFFAIR WITH YOUR HUSBAND BEFORE SOMEONE ELSE DOES

Copyright © 1987 by Susan Kohl and Alice Miller Bregman. All rights reserved. Printed in the United States of America. No part of this book may be used or reproduced in any manner whatsoever without written permission except in the case of brief quotations embodied in critical articles or reviews. For information, address St. Martin's Press, 175 Fifth Avenue, New York, N.Y. 10010

Library of Congress Catalog Card Number: 87-4434

ISBN: 0-312-91037-1   Can. ISBN: 0-312-91039-8

Printed in the United States of America

First St. Martin's Press mass market edition/June 1988

10 9 8 7 6 5 4 3 2 1

To my parents—still married after fifty-two years!
—AMB

To JLK—without whom . . . !
—SK

Contents

Acknowledgments

We want to thank the people whose support and contributions made this book possible: Ginger Barber, Werner Erhard, Jane Firth, Judith and Bob Shaw, and all the men and women who shared their lives, loves, and fantasies. A special thank you to Shirley Vanderhoff at the Westhampton Free Library for all her help. We used everything the library had to offer including the typewriter.

—Alice Miller Bregman and Susan Kohl

I want to thank my pals whose unfailing support and whose willingness to share their wisdom made it possible for me to get the job done:

Ellyn Ambrose, Margie Beebe, Meg Schneider Brodsky, Kate Ernst, Bonnie Hiller, Betty Kelly, Wendy Nicholson, Barbara Spector, Nealie and Jon Small, and Judith Yellin.

—AMB

While writing this book about love and relationships I looked often at my own relationships and was sustained by what I saw, what was available to me. There was my father's courage and grace no matter what the odds; my mother's joy and affirmation of life; my sons' humor and affection; my new daughter's warmth and spunk—each of them, Peter, David, Janice, loving, supportive, and willing to share their lives in their own special ways. I saw Howard and Elyse, a safe harbor, friends for fun or for tackling the tough times; Sara, wise beyond her years; Joanne, a supportive first reader; and Barberi, loving and generous. The people we call colleagues, my husbands' and mine, are part of the relationships I could count on. From all of them I learned about the joys of commitment and the power of intention. Without them there could not have been a book. Thank you.

—SK

HAVE A
LOVE
AFFAIR

WITH YOUR

HUSBAND

(Before Someone Else Does)

Introduction

This book is not for you if:

1. You'd rather get a divorce.
2. You think your marriage is perfect.

This book is for you if:

1. You remember a love affair as energizing, electrifying, and enlivening.
2. Ecstasy and enchantment have turned into calm and comfort in your marriage.
3. Sex is reserved for a Saturday night quickie and you never have sexy, scintillating Sundays.

If so, this book is exactly what you need. It will stimulate your imagination by opening up possibilities. There are suggestions for new ways to refresh your relationship, ways to create a new ambience for the two of you, and directions for how you can use the information you already have to make new decisions that will let you shake the doldrums, boredom, and the routines that develop within an enduring marriage.

This book may change how you view your life. Embarking on a love affair with your husband is the first step in reexamining the patterns of your behavior in order to have a satisfying marriage with a great sex life. This is likely to be surprising, sometimes uncomfortable, and always exhilarating. We know. That's how this book began—as a conversation between two friends that became an inquiry and led to great changes in both our lives.

One of us has been married for thirty years and calls her marriage a love affair; the other is in the middle of a love affair. By sharing our personal experiences and those of people we interviewed—what worked and what didn't, and the discussions about our own lives—how they are different, how they are the same—we think we can lead you to *Have a Love Affair With Your Husband* (Before Someone Else Does).

We met and became friends through work. We are very close in age and grew up in the fifties when everyone believed that marriage meant living happily ever after. Neither of us had any idea how that would happen. We were both in therapy at about the same time, both did the est training—at different times but with equal resistance and equally dramatic results. Once we recognized the similarities in our lives, we couldn't understand why our marriages had turned out so differently—one still married to the same man and the other divorced after five years. Since both of us said we wanted a lasting relationship with our husband, why did it work for one and not the other? Why did Kohl consider her relationship an ongoing love affair? Why didn't Bregman?

We began to interview each other. We wanted to find out why Alice got divorced and what has allowed Sue to stay married and continue to feel she has a successful relationship. Our conversation went on for years.

"I got married to the idea of marriage," Alice says, "and I loved being married. The man I married fit the basic specifications of the man I thought I should marry. That was good. But I never really focused on who he was. I think he may have been married to an idea too and didn't know who I was. It was a perfect match. We were married to marriage and not to each other. Perhaps many people behave in the same way. The lucky ones, after a time, begin to notice the person they married and are able to be with him or her instead of being married to their idea of marriage. My husband and I were never able to do that. And the ordinary events and issues that any couple encounter became insurmountable problems for us. Since it's almost impossible to live life committed to an idea instead of the person you're living with, we got divorced. Immediately I became the wronged wife whose marriage had failed. The failure I felt affected all my relationships, especially those with men. I began to think I was incapable of having a satisfying and lasting love affair and I was sure I would never remarry.

"When I met Sue, I thought her marriage had succeeded because she and her husband had qualities my husband and I lacked. They seemed generous with each other, open, good-humored, loving, even-tempered, fulfilled—in a word, perfect. I discovered that people with good marriages are, in fact, quite similar to everyone else. They have many desirable qualities along with all the undesirable ones. In another word, they're human. So how come Sue's marriage works and mine didn't really have a chance?"

"I have been married to the same man for thirty years," says Sue, "and if you had asked me fifteen years ago if our marriage would last that long, I would have said no. We had all the problems everyone had, and since we started out before there were endless articles on the subject, I had no idea how we could actually stay together and be happy. I think we were lucky and smart. We took what came up and used it to keep us together, rather than allow it to split us up. The basic ingredients in our relationship are enduring affection and, frankly, sex. We can always turn each other on. Well, almost always.

"But I know that wouldn't have been enough over the long haul if we hadn't been able to shift our perspectives, expectations, and attitudes.

"Would you believe that great realizations can come while cleaning out a closet? Well, mine did. I wasn't just cleaning out my closet, I was cleaning out my head. A good friend skilled in such matters was helping me, and as we examined the clothes I had held on to so stoutly (pun intended), she asked me to tell her the stories attached to them. I realized that not only had I kept skirts and pants that were too tight, I had also kept ideas and decisions about myself and my marriage that no longer fit. I realized I didn't have to keep old decisions any more than I had to keep old clothes. I was able to get rid of the clothing in a few days; it took longer to get rid of the old decisions.

* * *

"During the next days and then months, I thought about how often we make decisions unconsciously. And because we are unaware of them, it's difficult to change them, and they become powerful influences on our lives. I became aware that, in every area of my life, I held part of myself in reserve—I never gave a hundred percent. I thought it was too risky. I realized that because I was timid about showing my own sexuality, I held back; yet it's easier for me to start a fantasy and get him to play. I was embarrassed by my interest in sex, which made me timid; yet my interest— when I risk showing it—turns him on. I held back in other ways, too. When our children were young, it was easier for him to get time off to take a sick child to the doctor, and it turned out that he was better at organizing household activities than I, so I gave up being responsible for every-thing in the house, yet I thought I should protect him from the demands of small children. At the same time, I thought I was only qualified to work with children and that he was responsible for our financial well-being and I was responsi-ble for everything else. I wasn't aware of the decisions I'd made so there was no way for us to discuss them and dis-cover other ways of conducting our lives. By not giving a hundred percent because I thought it was too risky, I created a heavy burden for both of us! I started to experi-ment with new decisions about my clothes, my makeup, my job, my marriage. I began to be aware of my ideas about romantic love, sex, lust, and their place in my marriage. I realized that if I looked around a crowded room, my hus-band was the man I wanted. And, of course, he is the man I have. So I started to flirt with him. If I pretended we'd just met, he was happy to play along with me. He has always called me during the day to share a funny story, and every time I have a business meeting with a man he teases me—

he pretends he's jealous. He frequently introduces me to new people as "his old girl friend." I remembered how sexy and turned on he gets whenever we are in a hotel room—how he invites me into the shower, how many different ways he makes love. I also noticed how I turn myself off by focusing on what I don't like, on what I have to do tomorrow, or on just being tired. I realized I wanted him to be more romantic—my way. The acknowledgment I longed for had always been there. I'd just never noticed it. I started to listen to him in new ways and discovered it was no longer risky to be his partner, a hundred percent. I didn't have to hold anything in reserve. Our marriage began to have a roominess not present before.

"I hasten to add that we are still subject to life's irritations. We do not always please each other. We still argue, and are different people. (He is inclined to silence while mulling over a problem and I to excessive verbalization.) But there is a vigor and liveliness in our relationship that allows us to continue to bloom. Not bad for a thirty-year-old marriage!"

Alice's commitment to her idea of marriage (rather than the marriage itself) prevented her from experiencing a satisfying relationship. Sue's decision to discard outdated unconscious attitudes allowed her relationship to expand. Our conversations led us both to an understanding of how persistent ideas can be and how they can outlast their usefulness.

We began to look carefully at the disparity between the ideal picture of romance and marriage and its reality for most people. It became clear to us that outmoded ideas and decisions frequently prevent people from finding what they seek in the relationship they have. Instead, they long for something they don't have.

We can't prove it, but we believe that women provide the source that enriches relationships, though some men can and do provide it, too. For most men, devoting time and nurture to a relationship has not been a top priority (until recently); so far, women are more conscious about this. We also believe that when anyone examines the assumptions on which she (or he) builds relationships, her own insight allows for a shift in perspective thereby opening opportunities not understood before—including the possibility that a marriage should be ended. Since all assumptions are influenced by experiences and expectations, from time to time, it makes sense to reexamine them. In that way, we are able to make distinctions between feelings and emotions and the facts. Most of us get married with high hopes and expectations for happiness. To live life with no hope and low expectations is not much fun; a way of living we don't encourage.

This book can't change a marriage which should, in fact, be ended. Reading it might remind a woman in such a marriage of her strengths but it cannot take the place of proper counseling.

This book is an invitation to the woman who knows that the foundation of her marriage warrants a renewed commitment. It will help her to recapture the delicious aspects of her life with her husband and remind them of the agreements they made together. In the process, some of her decisions will become clear. And perhaps she'll find that she's ready to discard some of them.

We know it is possible to have it all—your calm, comfortable marriage plus the ecstasy and enchantment of having a love affair with your husband. Sue has it in her marriage, and Alice has it in her love affair. Achieving such a relationship isn't as difficult as it may seem. We're proof that you can have your marriage, and your affair, too.

Choose the One You Have

Who Are You?

Here you are. You're a relatively new wife. You had a delicious courtship that culminated in a divine wedding with parties and lots of gifts. Your work is going well. Your home is decorated. Your cooking gets better every day; your new husband loves it. And you are noticing that there is a remarkable absence of romance in your life.

Or you're a young mother with small children, and the only thing you have a lot of is dirty laundry. You have reached that infamous stage of life when even the sudden appearance of Mr. Clean or the White Tornado on your doorstep wouldn't faze you. Being too tired has become a way of life. There is certainly no romance in your days—never mind your nights.

Or you are a two-career couple. You earn more than he does, but whatever problem that may pose is eliminated when you balance your checkbook. As a result of the stresses and strains of your dynamic careers, you have noticed an absence of the old magic. Who has the time or energy for magic?

Or you've been married to the same wonderful man for umpteen years. He has more hair than you expected he would by now, he's moderately (or very) successful, your children are on track, and your parents are safely retired. You're living the American Dream—but where's the romance?

The Missing Something

Your life has most of the elements you planned for yourself some years ago. They may not look exactly the way you thought they would, and some elements may be absent, but basically, your life is fine. It works. Yet a little voice tells you that something you once had is missing. But what can you do about it?

You could redecorate or go back to school or change jobs. You could join a political club. You could organize a theater group, take up racquet ball, reread the classics or create a new project at work, look for a new place to live or have a baby. And when you've done all that, there will still be something missing from your life that you once had.

The pursuit of this missing element is the single most frequent cause of the breakup of marriages. The nicest, the most thoughtful, and the brightest people flip out and redo their lives in search of that precious commodity—the missing something that they once had. Most likely, the title of this book reminded you that before you got married, you were having a love affair. That's why you married the man you did. And that's not what seems to be going on between the two of you now.

The missing something in your life, the romance of your first days and nights together, is a dim memory. Clearly it's time to have a love affair. But the very idea of having an affair threatens everything you've worked for in your relationship. Besides, when you think of the available men you know you can't see how having an affair with any of them would help your marriage. However, if you give the matter some thought, you'll realize that you actually know the perfect man with whom to have an affair—your own husband.

A love affair with your husband will not incur lawyers' fees. Any ensuing emotional changes will not require psychiatric assistance for you, your husband, or your children. A love affair with your husband will not result in a nervous breakdown or new living arrangements.

The costs involved are entirely manageable (only some department store bills and a motel room or two). The time it takes and the modifications in your lifestyle are minimal. A love affair with your husband does not require keeping a secret calendar or making extraordinary arrangements for the kids. Best of all, a love affair with your own husband does not necessitate finding a suitable candidate. You've already committed yourself to him and plan to live with him for the rest of your life.

This book will remind you of how much you loved your husband in the first place; allow you to acknowledge that satisfying marriages require work; be a source for turning your fantasies into realities.

Having a love affair with your husband will also produce these benefits:

1. A new love affair is energizing—you'll feel so good you'll want to do more each day and with your life in general. It will inspire you. (The same is true for him.)
2. Since a love affair is energizing, you'll probably get a raise or a promotion or both.
3. Your husband will begin to believe that he really *is* something special, which is likely to lead to a raise or a promotion or a whole new business for him as well.
4. You will create an atmosphere that makes your children radiate well-being.
5. Your friends will adore being around you and want to know your secret. Don't tell them. Give them this book.
6. You will rediscover all the qualities that made you want to marry him in the first place.
7. It will confirm your original judgment—you *did* marry the right man after all.
8. Who could ask for anything more?

A word of warning: You will have to put aside the girl you were and let him get to know the woman you have become. This means admitting that love and sex deserve time and attention and deciding that you are going to do something about it.

Most people don't think that love affairs can be created —in a marriage or anywhere else—but that they just happen. Love affairs are usually associated with the carefree single life or with clandestine relationships. We believe that anyone can create a romantic affair. The key is you must be willing to play—the same way you play any game—for the fun of it. After all, games are not life-and-death struggles, they are only games. So if you're willing to play Trivial Pursuit and be wrong or not know the answer, you'll enjoy the game even if you lose. When you play tennis, if you're willing to miss a good shot, you'll have a decent game no matter what the score is. If you don't play that way, you're not going to have a good time because you'll be taking it too seriously; and you'll be making it more difficult to win because you've used up too much energy on the possibility of losing. At the same time, when you become expert at something—cooking or tennis or aerobics or writing—you feel good about yourself, and these good feelings permeate your whole life. Since you know you'll be married to this man for many more years, you really risk nothing by playing a new game with him. And if you play well, the good feelings will be boundless.

In order to have a love affair with your own (familiar) husband you need to recapture your interest in him as a lover. Tim Gallwey, in his book *Inner Tennis: Playing the Game,* states that boredom interferes with our ability to perceive and respond to whatever we experience. Our minds tell us that we know exactly what to expect in familiar situations so instead of being open to an experience we tend to categorize it in advance and we don't notice the reality. We create our own self-fulfilling prophecies. "All things common, ordinary, continual, frequent, and obvious in time become barely noticed by the mind, which comes to assume that it knows all about them. So thinking, it loses its natural curiosity and attentiveness and therefore its awareness." If you've been married to the same man for some period of time, chances are you've lost your ability to see him as a new experience. Your mind has predetermined his every action and has stopped paying attention.

So, the first step in this process is to decide to have a love affair with your husband, to choose him again. Make this decision the same way you decide to do anything. Once you have, you will begin to demonstrate it because our decisions do inform our actions. (If you decide *not* to have a love affair with your husband, don't worry about it. Just read on and live vicariously.)

A New Focus

We always forget that each of us sees the world through our own eyes and not through anyone else's. Furthermore, our perceptions are shaped by our expectations. Everyone sees things in his or her own way; no one can stand in anyone else's shoes and share the same angle of vision. But all of us can move two steps in any direction and achieve a new view. By shifting your angle of vision, you can illuminate the ordinary events in your life so that new possibilities come into focus—possibilities that would not have been apparent from any other vantage point.

Haven't you ever been surprised at some of the stories people tell about their romances? Or at the way some people choose to live, to vacation, even to work? For instance, the couple who met and fell in love at first sight in a laundromat will always recall that place as special and may continue to do the laundry as a way of spending time together. If one couple can feel romantic over laundry, can anyone else feel that way? Many people do not realize how much they control their own view points. As an experiment, could you shift your point of view and find something romantic about washing his clothes? Perhaps you're thinking, "Laundry? Really, this is ridiculous!" However, we've used this example because it sounds so farfetched. So think about it. If you can shift your point of view about laundry, isn't it possible you could have a new point of view about many other, more significant things in your life?

When we feel dissatisfied with our lives, most of us want to change what's in them—including the people. In fact, we usually identify the people who are closest to us as the source of our dissatisfaction.

"If only my kids didn't make so much noise, I'd be able to concentrate better."

"If only my husband came home on time, we'd be able to eat dinner at a normal hour and get to bed earlier. In a better mood, I might want to make love more often—or he would."

"If only he made more money, we could——"(You fill in the blank).

"If only he told me he loved me more often, I'd feel better."

But trying to change other people is as hopeless as trying to ensure that your husband will never produce any dirty laundry! It is much easier to change our point of view about our lives than to change the circumstances or the people in them. It's just as hard to truly change yourself (could you stop producing dirty laundry?) as it is anyone else. But it is not impossible to shift your point of view. All you need to do is allow yourself a new focus. Of course, this new focus will include the old familiar one—you will still have dirty laundry—but as a human being, you are not limited to only one angle of vision. You can have both the old and the new at the same time.

The Power of Observation

The way to move to a new point of view is to first become aware of your beliefs and biases. These include your feelings, opinions, body sensations and the judgments you make about what you have in your life. You need not take any action while you're doing this, simply take notice. In the process, you might feel irritated, amused, surprised, pleased, dissatisfied, or good—just allow yourself to notice. You can experiment when you go to bed tonight. Notice what happens when your husband gets into bed. How does he let you know he wants to make love? Does he make you feel like doing it, too? Or does he make you feel like it's one more household chore to be done before sleeping? What are your reactions to him? What are your reactions if he doesn't and you want him to? Notice your breathing and his. Notice the tone and quality of your voice and his. Notice if the room smells a certain way. Notice if you do. Notice if he does.

Since objective observation enables you to distance yourself from your reactions, inevitably you have now changed your focus. The minute something is further away, you see it differently—you see more of it, it's smaller and less significant, but it's still there. Your husband is still going to make his usual move indicating that he wants to make love, but your take on it will have changed. (For a graphic demonstration of how your focus changes your point of view, turn on the TV and put your nose to the screen. What can you see? Now, pull back slowly from the screen. Notice how much more of the picture you can see. Notice how your perspective has changed.)

The philosopher Robert C. Solomon writes in his book *Love, Emotion, Myth and Metaphor* that each of us chooses to feel romantic love—it doesn't choose us. We think Solomon is right: We can choose to feel romantic just as we can choose to change our focus. Furthermore, if we can choose to feel romantic and choose our point of view, we can also choose the people on whom to focus. You chose to marry your husband in the first place. Now choose him again. Don't add any expectations to your choice. Don't think about whether or not it's possible to be swept off your feet like you were when you first met. Don't think about what you do or don't like about him. Don't make any assumptions at all. Just choose him.

2

What Is a Love Affair?

The Perfect Love Affair

The perfect love affair begins during a sun-drenched afternoon in some gorgeous place—San Francisco or a white, sandy beach in the middle of the summer. The sky is brilliant blue and cloudless, the colors look pure and rich. The sun warms your body and his from the outside in. Your feelings for each other warm your bodies from the inside out. Wordlessly, your mouths touch—softly at first, so that you can feel the velvety smoothness of each other's lips; then, as you taste the warmth of each other's mouths, you press your bodies closer. The kisses are warm and sweet, and like rich, dark chocolate, you want more—it is irresistible. The warmth now envelopes the two of you like a cocoon—the city or the beach disappears. There are only the two of you in a delicious embrace. As you enfold each other and the warmth flows to your arms and legs, your thoughts dissolve and you become the other. Now, there is only one hot eager body moving in perfect harmony. There are no more judgments: Is he the one? Should I let him? Will she want me? What about dinner? What about next week or tomorrow or an hour from now? None of that matters. Only the sensations of skin on skin and muscles tightening matter. Your legs feel longer and stronger and more graceful, your bodies feel lithe and young, your arms are filled with boundless strength. You are beautiful. He is lovely and loving and lovable. It is bliss. And then you are two bodies again—warm and sweaty and exhilarated. You talk about something important or say nothing at all and you stroke each other gently, easing the moment of physical separation. At five P.M. you once again notice the sun drenched afternoon. You have a glass of wine. You shower. You dress slowly. You kiss again as you pass each other doing these routine activities. Just before you put on your last article of clothing, you hug tightly, allowing your bodies to remember each other. You are dressed. You're back in real life.

When was the last time you had an afternoon like that with your husband? Was it when you were having a love affair? How can you create similar romantic interludes in your marriage? In order to deliberately create a love affair, you have to know what it is. If you don't know what it is, and you've been married to the same man for five years or ten or even fifty, how can you, or any of us, make it happen?

The Dynamics of a Love Affair

How do you define the elements of a love affair? How many of us have ever taken the time to analyze the separate pieces? We think to do so would ruin its most important aspect—its spontaneity. If we look too closely, we're sure the magic will disappear.

Our research included group meetings with women of all ages, we had conversations with men, and we interviewed experts in sex therapy, family and marriage counseling, and several psychiatrists and psychologists with a variety of points of view and experience. We read everything from Alexandra Penney's *Great Sex* to Robert C. Solomon's philosophical inquiry into the nature of love. (See the bibliography for our complete recommended reading list.)

Common to all love affairs are certain characteristics, chief among them the element of surprise. No one expects to fall in love. Though every blind date may be the love of your life, it's surprising when he, or she, is. Can you remember what was unexpected and surprising about falling in love with your husband?

Secrecy is another aspect all love affairs share. Some are illicit as well. Not that we necessarily meet in secret, but until we're sure, we keep our feelings a secret. "After all," we reason, "what if it doesn't work out? What if no one else can see what I see in him?" What was the secret or illicit element in your romance with your husband? Was it the time you spent with him when you should have been somewhere else? Or was it what you actually did when you were together?

Once launched, a love affair has a life of its own. It is irresistible, impossible to ignore or slow down or stop. One of the great pleasures of having an affair is sharing its nuances: its texture, tone, and ambience. Everything is described, even tasted and touched in a special way. The candles illuminating a dinner for two are experienced differently than those we use because a fuse blew.

People in love describe the object of their affection in terms that are larger than life: "I've never met anyone with such green, green eyes," says a woman in her twenties of her new love. "She is the most beautiful and sexy woman in the world," says a man in his thirties of his latest amour.

For most lovers, the details of where, when, and how are all-consuming, and the most mundane conversation or place is elevated to mythic proportions: "On our last night in the hotel in St. Louis, we were too tired to go out for dinner so we ordered from room service," reports a twenty-eight-year-old woman describing the beginning of her affair with an Italian journalist. "We had the most exciting evening—the tablecloth was the perfect shade of pink, and there was a bud vase with a beautiful deep-pink rose in it. My club sandwich was the best I've ever tasted, and he looked handsome and sexy sitting across from me eating his chef salad. Then we watched a terrible dubbed porn movie (that wasn't even hot). Oh, it was simply the best evening we'd spent together. We loved it!"

Women having a love affair experience their bodies totally differently: they feel taller, slimmer yet rounder, and fuller; their skin seems smoother; their senses become more acute. What is it that you notice about your sexuality? Can you smell your own perfume? Are you more aware of your breasts? Your nipples? Does the silky feel of your underwear arouse you as you move?

From our interviews it was clear that people in the midst of a love affair see, hear, smell, taste, and feel everything more keenly—they are alive in every fiber of their being.

They daydream about being together when they are apart, and when they are together, they fantasize about being together again. They can see only the beloved's virtues; faults (if they are noticed at all) are charming, endearing foibles.

We met with psychiatrist Robert Shaw and his wife, therapist Judith Shaw, co-directors of the Family Institute, Berkeley, California, in May 1985. Our interview extended over several hours and gave us the opportunity to learn what drives some couples into counseling and how these couples differ from those who consider their marriages satisfying. The Shaws told us that those characteristics that one finds so appealing and important at the start of an affair are usually those most likely to become the source of our greatest discontent when we take off the rose-colored glasses. A man who displays independence and self-sufficiency in the early stages of a romance is admired; later on, he can be perceived of as aloof and uncaring.

When Does a Love Affair Stop Being Romantic and Become a Marriage? (Or The Prince Turns Into a Frog)

The first casualty of marriage is indeed the rose-colored glasses. For some, marriage means the end of heroic sexual exploits. They no longer push their bodies beyond human endurance and they rarely, if ever, discuss their love making. They're sure their love affair is over, never to be rekindled. According to Robert and Judith Shaw, people don't stop to examine their lives until things aren't working. Then they go for counseling or get divorced or both. In the

Shaws' experience, happily married couples describe their marriages in very similar terms as those who don't feel their relationship is working. For example, if asked "Do you get hugged enough?" both couples will respond "no." The difference is that in good marriages no one decides that not being hugged enough is cause for divorce. In bad marriages someone might use such a behavior—or the lack of it—to reinforce their own negative view of their marriage. They add this to the evidence they are collecting of their failed relationship. The conclusion they come to—divorce—is an altogether different outcome of the same situation experienced by a happily married couple.

"It is the secondary thoughts one has about the event that make the difference," the Shaws told us.

Secondary thoughts are the ones expressed by the little voices in your head. For people in good marriages, the thought that follows "I don't get hugged enough" is "oh, well, maybe I'm not hugging enough myself" or "but think of all the other wonderful things he or she does." For people in bad marriages, the secondary thought might be, "I don't have to take this kind of behavior, I deserve to be treated better. I'll find somebody else."

The "secondary thoughts" of people in bad marriages are judgmental and condemning, so it is impossible for them to figure out how to fix their relationship. When we are in love, we are operating on our most positive impulses. We are forgiving and magnanimous with everyone. We are hard put to find fault with our lovers and are quite adept at finding excuses for behaviors that are unacceptable at other times. If you were having a love affair with your husband before you got married, did you think that he hugged you enough then? Perhaps he still does but you don't "describe" it in the same way now.

"There are two dimensions present in all our lives," according to the Shaws. "What is actually happening, and how we describe what has happened; the experience we have and how we describe that experience." This analysis was confirmed by our interviews. When people are asked to describe romance and love, their responses are very conventional. Television and the movies have so homogenized our romantic images that everyone goes on automatic and gives the same answers. Mention love and romance and most people say, "Moonlight, roses, champagne and caviar, elegant black tie for him, low-cut, shimmering long dresses for her, gleaming silver and sparkling crystal." There are some variations: wood-burning fireplaces, candlelight, ski slopes, tropical beaches, and, occasionally, a country inn. None of these is exactly the setting of everyday life, and for the few who live that way, such scenes become ordinary.

We discovered that the well-learned lessons from Hollywood movies (which we all agree have little to do with anyone's real life—including Hollywood stars. No one can tell us that the lives Joanne Woodward and Paul Newman lead at home in Connecticut resemble in any way the characters they've played on the silver screen) are the basis for our images of "happily ever after."

When people are asked to describe their most romantic moments, the events may be ordinary, but their descriptions are not. For example, one woman related her most romantic moment this way: "I knew he was the one and we would get married when he invited me to have a beer with him. We were in college, he was in a fraternity, I had never met anyone like him before." As she described this truly ordinary event, her demeanor changed: her eyes lit up, she smiled broadly, she looked like the twenty-year-old she was at the time.

Think about it! How many romantic moments have you had on that moonlit beach or star-kissed slope? Did he actually propose over a candlelit dinner in that perfect cafe? Did he seduce you by sweeping you into his arms and telling you that he had to have you, and then did he carry you up the stairs to a satin-swathed bower? No?

Some love affairs begin in laundromats, in telephone booths, at airports, in financial workshops, at the supermarket. In other words, during the pedestrian activities and mundane places in which we all find ourselves. Location is not important.

How do you describe your most romantic moment? How do you feel about it now? How does it fit into your images of a perfect marriage? How is it different? How long does it take for the formerly magnificent to be reduced once more to the merely mundane? How often can one gasp with delight over the face and form of the one who is always there? That state of exquisite sexual tension is hard to maintain when the baby is crying or you have to get up at five-thirty A.M. to make a plane. There is no question that the rose-colored glasses are shattered before the first anniversary. However, since a love affair can begin anywhere, anytime, you can begin your affair with your husband right now, wherever you are.

When Our Images Don't Match Our Realities

Most women agree that they want romance to be an integral part of their lives—no matter what. But, in fact, their most romantic moments did not include silk, satin, champagne, or glitter. Their experiences had personal significance and rarely fit anyone else's description of "romantic." Furthermore, the women we interviewed revealed a startling gap between their romantic images and their everyday lives—a discrepancy they failed to perceive. We did. And we also noticed that, instead of revising their notions of "romance," they condemn their own realities. When people condemn their current lives, they invalidate their past as well. Marriages are based on a shared past.

Robert C. Solomon believes that a love affair evokes a search for a shared past as we try to find ways we might have met or places we might have been. We seek common ground in the music we love, the people we know, the food we enjoy, how we spend vacations—in everything we like. In the middle of a love affair we project a shared future. We plan our tomorrows, starting with the next time we'll be together to ways we can escape our everyday existence.

Husbands and wives already share a future. Sue used their shared past as a foundation for their future; Alice condemned their past and therefore couldn't see a positive future. And she totally forgot how good her husband had looked through the rose-colored tint of their earlier love affair.

Since the rosy glow did exist once, it is possible to access the old, heroic descriptions, and to tap into the shared memories. But first you have to remember. People who have been married for a while know how to create sexual and sensual delights for each other. Their familiar places and usual situations can again be the setting of a love affair because they were, once. Tim Gallwey says, "Sometimes I play a game called, 'I've never met my wife before.' It is difficult but rewarding, and its object is to forget as many of the concepts—both negative and positive—that I have accumulated about Sally as I can. I try to forget I have ever seen her before. By this I don't mean that I act as I would when first meeting someone; rather, I simply let go of all the categories I hold in my mind about her, and when she says or does something I don't put what I hear or see into preconceived pigeonholes. When I succeed in this exercise, I am perceiving Sally in the present, and it's a fresh and lively experience. It's also hard to describe, but it's as different from my usual perception of her—from relating to her through the inevitable collections of thought, emotions, and past impressions that one accumulates about people they see frequently—as day from night."

Pretend You've Never Seen Him Before

Tonight when you are in bed with your husband, pretend you've never seen him before. Notice how it feels to have his body next to yours. Notice its warmth, the texture of his skin, if he has a hairy chest. Notice your place in the bed, and his place. Be aware of how close you are and how far apart. What part of his body do you want to touch? What part of your body would you like him to touch? Or do you just want to go to sleep? Notice that, too. Notice how easy it would be to move closer to him if you chose to. Remember how much you've enjoyed him in the past. Remember that you chose him in the first place.

Let your body remember that you chose him. Let your body remember how it fits with his. Trust it—it does remember. It remembers the love affair you once had.

3

Remembering

You were there when you first met. Remember? You could hardly bear to be apart. There was an incredible sense of urgency to every meeting, even if you had just been together all day or all night. Everything he did was important to you. You talked about him to your friends. You planned and fantasized about your life together. When you became lovers you were in an exalted state of expectation —all the time. You couldn't get enough of each other. You fell asleep exhausted, sated, and yet you woke up with an incredible need. This sense of urgency was present in everything you did, thought, imagined, or planned. It swept you toward the inevitable—getting married.

Start remembering the love affair you had with your husband before you were married. Recall the moments of romance, passion, lust, and joy you shared. As you remember, remind your husband so that his memory will be stimulated too and you can reminisce together.

Jane discovered the power of remembering during the weekly drives out to the country house she shares with her husband, Michael—a trip notorious for its bumper-to-bumper traffic and seemingly endless tedium. She started by asking some questions about their early days together. At first it sounded as if she knew something he might have forgotten, sort of a test he might fail, so she rephrased her questions. She wanted to have fun, not start an argument.

"When we borrowed Harvey's car to park at the Olentangy River, did you have to pay him?" Jane asked.

Michael shrugged. "I just had to put gas in the car."

"Do you remember how fast the car windows would fog up and how the cops would shine their flashlights in our faces?"

They went on that way for a while; then Jane asked, "Do you want to know why I'm asking all these questions?"

"No," Michael said, grinning, "but don't stop."

You don't have to wait for just the right moment before you reminisce with your husband. You can do it anywhere —even in such a mundane place as the car in the middle of a traffic jam—anytime—even on the way to work. Engage your husband in the game. He'll like it as much as Michael did.

Remember, the Man You Married Is the One You Chose

Our memories are stored in the same part of the brain responsible for sexual desire. It is called the "limbic system." These memories can be called up at will or stimulated involuntarily by something similar and familiar—a scent of perfume or an aroma of food, the sound of music or a voice, the sight of some place or person, or a particular activity. (The limbic system is also the storehouse for old angers and resentments. More about these in Chapter 4.)

What you were doing in your life when you chose your husband may seem a blur at first. But if you think about it for a while you will be able to recall what you looked like then, what he looked like, and the moment you knew he might be the one. Remember?

We invited a number of women to a meeting, the purpose of which was to discuss love and romance. We asked them to recall the moment they knew their husband was "the one."

"Jay and I had known each other for several years because we were in related businesses," a forty-year-old advertising executive told us. "We bumped into each other at a party I hadn't expected to attend. I remember that there was something different about the way we greeted each other—something shifted between us. I could almost see it move, and I realized that our relationship was about to change. And it did. Later, Jay reminded me that we had danced together when we were at the same convention in Dallas several years earlier. 'Where did you disappear to after we danced?' he asked me. 'We could have started this sooner.' I remember what I was wearing when we met at that party. I remember what he was drinking and who was there, and I certainly remember how I felt—elated! Thanks for asking me to remember."

Remembering that the man you married is the one you chose is something you can do anywhere, anytime, no matter what else you're doing. Try it while you are brushing your teeth. You are likely to find the experience so delightful even your chores will be more enjoyable.

"I thought he was handsome, sexy, and terrifically purposeful about what he was going to do with his life," Linda recalled. "I was sure that being married to him would be perfect for me and I was ready to do anything to make that happen. I lived in a state of heightened tension—it was bliss when we were together and torment when we were apart. I guess my feelings were perfectly balanced. I was always daydreaming about how our lives would be—like a combination of *Gone With the Wind* and that Finney/Hepburn movie, *Two for the Road.* I guess it didn't turn out quite that way. Actually, it turned out better."

Barbara, married to a man who had a young son from a previous marriage, recalled how their first months together were marked by total intimacy and sharing, then sudden and abrupt emotional withdrawal. "We would spend ten days together, squeezing in all our daily activities—working, seeing his son Timmy, going to classes. We'd spend the rest of the time either in passionate positions or in passionate discourse about the rest of our lives. Suddenly, I would feel completely overwhelmed. He had so many obligations and responsibilities. I wasn't sure I wanted to take them on. And he felt the same way. We would have conversations about 'space,' about not seeing each other for a while. But we couldn't stay away from each other, no matter what we said or thought."

When people start recalling the moments of choosing, it always sounds as if they had no choice. Robert and Judith Shaw confirm this. Their research shows that once people "choose," the relationship is irresistible. There is indeed no choice.

Recall How You Couldn't Keep Your Hands Off Him

Did you meet your husband in the days of hot and heavy petting, making out, or whatever it was called then? Or did you two meet later when there were fewer restrictions? Whenever you met him, do you remember how much you wanted to touch him?

"He had a great body and wore elegant, well-tailored clothes. When we went out I wanted to look as perfect as he did and then we would spend the whole time talking about taking off our clothes," Lisa recalled. "I think it was particularly exciting to see this elegant man get messed up because he lusted after me. In fact, I still like to start making love fully clothed and wake up in the morning to find a tangled trail of silk tie, pantyhose, and underwear."

Louise remembers walking down the street with him, always managing to touch him somewhere, somehow. She remembers the first dinners with their parents when they could only play "footsie."

Joan remembers sitting on his lap or curling up next to him and discovering the incredible softness of his earlobe.

"Friends of mine had a dinner party and he was one of the guests," Anne reminisced. "I knew he was interested in me from the first moment we met. It gave the dinner party a special tone, an excitement, to know that something was going to happen as a result of our both being there. And something did—we've been married for twenty-four years, had three children, developed careers, and moved twenty-five hundred miles from our original homes." She laughed.

"Can you imagine what would have happened if one of us hadn't gone to that dinner party?"

When you couldn't keep your hands off him you were eager to let him know how you felt. Remember? Are you willing to let him know now?

Recall How He Couldn't Keep His Hands Off You

Did you meet your husband when almost all dancing was slow dancing? Some of us called it "The Grind," others, "The Fish"; now, it's called "slow dancing." In those days, it was the only legitimate reason to be in each other's arms in public. The fact that you were dancing, moving slowly to music, was almost irrelevant. There were so many taboos that we needed slow dancing to find out if there was any electricity between us. And when there was, wow!

Dee remembers slow dancing. "His urgency, that unmistakable bulge in his trousers was so enticing. Knowing he responded that way to me was such a turn on. And, you know, I still love to dance—so does he."

"We would make out for hours, touch each other everywhere," Terry mused. "He unlocked my body for me. Until him, I hadn't really discovered it."

Do you remember the first three hundred times you made love? Discovering the nooks and crannies of each other's bodies? That exquisite sexual tension that surfaced no matter how often it was sated? The way it felt to be wet from each other's sweat?

When he couldn't keep his hands off you, you were always turned on. Remember?

Remember How Much It Meant When You Found Out That You Loved Each Other

Do you remember how thrilled you were when you realized that he was the one—and that he loved you too? You were "it" for him. You heard it in his voice and saw it on his face. It was apparent in the way he showed you off, in how he wanted you to see his favorite places. It was part of the gifts he gave you, roses at the office, birthstone earrings, silly but sweet Valentines, the gestures he made that surprised even him.

Elizabeth remembers that one day they started to talk about names for children and what they would be doing next year and the year after that. She can't remember how they decided to get married, and she's sure he never asked her directly. They just started to make up stories about their life together.

Nancy recalls how insistent he was that she spend all her free time with him, how suddenly there were so many people to meet, friends, family, even his boss. She remembers how he wanted to tell her everything he knew about wines and all about his favorite musicians. He wanted her to know all about him.

*　　*　　*

When you found out that you loved each other something was happening between you, remember?

Reminisce With Your Husband

There is a nostalgic quality about reminiscing. Usually it happens easily and naturally with friends we haven't seen in a while. So reminisce, not as a test to see if he remembers things the way you do, but rather as a spur to stimulate memories.

Betty found herself thinking about the way she and her husband (then lover) used to spend weekends. Together they would race through the Saturday chores—cleaners, laundry, supermarket—to be free for an afternoon movie. Then, they would eat pizza, Chinese, or spaghetti, buy the Sunday papers, and spend the rest of the weekend in bed. When she recalled this to her husband he added his own memories. She used to bring juice, coffee, and English muffins to bed and they would lie on the crumbs all day not minding at all. Finally they would crawl out for a shower (which they took together) and a proper meal.

"When I asked him if he'd like to spend a weekend like that now if I could get my mother to take the kids, he actually offered to call her himself," Betty laughingly told us.

"We used to leave notes for each other in the funniest places," Beth recalled. "My favorite was his raincoat pocket. Thinking up the most imaginative places became a contest. Larry considered his winning move the inside of a hamper we only used for picnics. I didn't find it for eight months. When I realized the endless possibilities open to me now that we live in a six-room house, I put a new note behind the light bulbs in the utility room. Larry countered with one wrapped around the wire of the blender. We have started our old game again, and it is great fun."

What ritual from those days can you re-create now? Pick something you both remember with pleasure, and you will be well on your way to a fulfilling love affair with your husband.

As you reminisce, pay attention to what is happening in your body. Memories are not only in the mind's eye but the ears, nose, pit of the stomach, in your arms and legs and all those lovely secret places. It is impossible to think about something you once felt without beginning to feel it again.

Tina, married for over twenty years, described how important her sense of smell is. "Not only can I instantly evoke my favorite aunt by a mere whiff of perfume, but all my memories include a description of the way things smelled. The dorm I lived in, the movie theater we went to when we were in college, the first car we had, the shampoo I used. When I remembered the shampoo, I actually went out to find it. Regretfully, Revlon did not care as much for the scent of the original Aquamarine as I did, and they've changed the formula—or my memory is faulty. But it was fun to look for it."

Marlene and her husband began their romance in a very narrow single bed. It was covered with a tartan-plaid throw. As she thought about that old bed, she realized that her children's pram blanket was the same plaid, and that was probably why she bought it. She dug it out of the storage closet and put it on the sofa in the den. As soon as her husband saw it, he recognized it. "Is that the blanket from our old twin bed?" he asked. He was grinning from ear to ear. "And did we have a good time that evening!" Marlene reported.

Now, remember a specific day or evening when you and your husband were newly aware of each other as lovers. What season of the year was it? Were you wearing something new? Something special? Do you remember how pleased you were by your appearance and by his? Can you recall how your clothes felt on your body? Think about where you were and why. Were you riding up to the country to meet some of his friends? Were you in your first apartment or his? Did you use a special perfume or shampoo in those days? Do you remember how good he smelled? And how close together you sat? What music did you listen to?

What turned you on and into lovers in the first place still has the same power; it is still stored in your limbic system. Allow yourself to reexperience it. Share your memories with your husband. You'll both feel good.

Feeling Good

It is six o'clock. The day is over. It's time to refresh yourself before the evening. You allow yourself the luxury of a bubble bath or a long, hot shower. Even though you have nothing special planned, you decide to do something different with your hair and to put on elaborate makeup. Maybe you'll even put on a dress or a housecoat whose fabric will feel wonderful next to your skin. So what if you and your husband are going to eat hamburgers with the kids and then watch a basketball game. You allow yourself to feel the water cascading against your body. You take extra time putting moisturizer on your legs because you are suddenly aware of how soft and smooth your skin is—and you like it. You decide to use your most expensive perfume— the one you reserve for important occasions. You put on your best, lacy underpants and decide to skip the bra. You put on a silk blouse and your most comfortable jeans instead of a dress. You choose sparkling earrings. You allow yourself to feel slightly out of character and have fun anyway. You are almost finished putting on your makeup when your husband comes home and finds you in front of the mirror. You decide to tell him what a good time you're having and how great you feel. You ask his opinion on your eye shadow. Your good mood is irresistible and, uncharacteristically, he catches your spirit and tells you to add some glitter. You use the gold eye-liner pencil you bought last year and haven't touched. "Perfect," he approves. And you both go into the kitchen to make the hamburgers. The kids notice that something is different—it doesn't matter that they don't know exactly what—and stop arguing. You all have dinner together, and it feels like a party instead of Wednesday.

When you got married, no one told you that ninety-eight percent of your attention would be focused on the mundane details of everyday life: garbage, shopping, laundry, car pools, lessons, meetings, packing, and on and on. In fact, how many wives complain when their husbands don't compliment them anymore, don't remember their birthdays or anniversaries, don't send them flowers, and have forgotten how they used to have fun together—how they played? Most don't even notice. Once you've learned to live without romance, the freshness, vitality, and energy of a love affair seems totally remote from marriage—until now.

Leftovers: Resentment, Anger, No Sex

Once you've begun remembering how it used to be, you can't help noticing that it isn't like that now. A not uncommon response to this observation is resentment: you may feel cheated of those intensely pleasurable feelings you had when you were first in love and couldn't keep your hands off each other. Resentments are generally hard to hide and are expressed as annoyance or full-blown rage. Many people are incapable of allowing their rage to explode so that it can dissipate; instead, it leaks out in subtle ways, often at inappropriate times.

If you haven't found a safe way to express your anger and resentment, if you haven't admitted how much you miss the compliments and the flowers, it is likely that you do not feel very good about yourself. If you've taken special care to make yourself attractive at the end of the day, and then your husband comes home and doesn't notice, you'll probably feel pretty mad at him. If you don't express your anger appropriately, it will be even more difficult to feel ready and responsive later when he gets into bed and wants to make love.

Simmering, repressed rage is a burden first for you and then, because it is so heavy, for all the people in your life. And one of the most common places to unload it—at least some of it—is in bed. Denying your husband sex seems the perfect way to get back at him for depriving you. "He's not giving me much pleasure these days, why should I try to please him?" Most of us deny ever having had such a mean idea—we're much too sophisticated, liberated, experienced. Because it's unacceptable and we can't admit that's how we feel, we find other, more subtle ways to express our resentment. Since it's so much easier to blame another than ourselves, we try to find fault with our husbands. "Obviously," you tell yourself, "the reason you don't like the way he says 'let's do it' is because he's lost his smoothness, he takes you for granted, he's not romantic anymore. He's changed." And you don't like it. You've forgotten that he's *always* done it that way, and it used to be just fine. In fact, he may not have changed at all. What has changed is the way you feel about it. You've allowed your unexpressed rage and resentment to color your feelings and responses to him.

Your husband may also have some repressed anger that leaks out of him at inappropriate times. Yet it rarely becomes an issue at bedtime: most men do not withhold sex to get even with women. It is primarily women who use sex to work through their anger. Husbands are not changed— or marital problems solved—by their wife's sexual withdrawal. Men don't like it, they don't get it, and usually they don't put up with it. They go looking for "someone who understands," making a real problem out of what was probably a simple (and solvable) dissatisfaction.

Such behavior will hardly produce a love affair with your husband. But it will guarantee someone else's affair with him, or, at the least, make you the butt of those awful jokes about headaches!

Rather than ignoring your anger, take a look at it. If you express it directly and appropriately, you provide a way for the two of you to discuss the problem and clear a path for your husband to examine his behavior (and you yours) which, in turn, creates an opportunity for change and compromise.

On Having Arguments

Nobody having a love affair is ever angry or fights, right? Alas, wrong. And in a marriage there are plenty of opportunities for disagreements, arguments, and outright battles. Unfortunately, most people have difficulty dealing with anger—it is the least acceptable of all our emotions. Instead, we choose not to express our anger, turn it inward and, as a result, become depressed. It is less risky than expressing our rage. That could mean confrontation, and then perhaps we'd have to fight. Since anger and fear—whether expressed or repressed—cause dramatic physiological reactions, it is important for our well-being to know how to deal with them.

Willard Gaylor, in *The Rage Within, Anger in Modern Life*, describes fear and anger as "only part of complex emotional responses which mobilize an individual for action." These responses were originally designed to help us survive—not to protect our pride or dignity. Since we no longer trek through the wilds alert for predators, a "fight or flight" response isn't necessary most of the time. Still, it persists. Gaylor contends that the first survival technique apparent in infants is not "fight or flight" but what he calls "clutch and cling," a response manifesting itself in adulthood as "abandonment and isolation." We don't have to be rejected or abandoned literally to experience a "clutch and cling" response. The mere suggestion that we are unlovable or unworthy frequently triggers it, and we show our fear by getting angry, as if our very survival were, indeed, threatened.

"Given the residual association of love and survival," Gaylor writes, "and given the fact that most of us operate in a world of assumptions that are never tested, suggestions

42

of our unlovability or our unworthiness invariably are perceived as a threat and will be met with fear and anger. The reality that operates on our physiology is the perceived reality, not a measure of the actual world." Thus we get trapped in a vicious circle: what we perceive may trigger either the "clutch and cling" or "fight or flight" response, and we generally respond in a way guaranteed to provoke anger and fear in another. In the end, we have done an excellent job of making reality match our perceptions. How many fights begin because we've misinterpreted what someone else said, or worse, what they thought? And how frequently in marriage do we make false assumptions—based on how well we think we know the other person—that in turn lead to battles royal because our partner behaved in a way we assumed he wouldn't?

"I hated the fights Dan and I used to have," Marge recalled. "They were so intense, and they lasted for days, and I used to feel so threatened. I was and am still able to evoke the most impressive rage from him. And when he gets angry, he says horrible things. I used to believe every word he uttered, and the last words out of his mouth were always, 'Why don't you just leave!' I thought he meant it. I'd imagine myself bereft of everything—no children, no home, no money, no way to earn a living, and I'd become despondent. He'd get over his rage in about twenty-four hours while I was left deeply depressed. I'd allow myself to get angry only when it seemed safe. So every argument followed a pattern and lasted a minimum of forty-eight hours, sometimes longer. During that time I'd also feel guilty about being angry or about having done something to make Dan mad at me. I also resented him for saying such awful things and was just as irked that I believed them. Being angry was not okay with me.

"Finally, I began to realize that Dan didn't mean everything he said in the heat of the moment. It was just the way he expressed his anger. When I understood that, I stopped being so afraid and, as a result, I didn't get so depressed. After a while, I could even be objective enough to figure out why, from his point of view, he had gotten so angry in the first place. Because I felt less threatened, I didn't take it all as intensely as I used to, and I could begin to understand how Dan felt. Not too long ago, I actually suggested to him that since we both knew we were going to forgive each other, perhaps we could speed up the process so that our fights would last a few hours instead of two or three days. Of course, he pretended not to know what I was talking about. But the net result is that now we can get over our anger in a much shorter time."

As Marge discovered, it is possible to redirect the way two people quarrel. It requires that only one of them be conscious of the patterns. The key is to observe the process and collect some information on which you can act. The next time you get angry don't stop yourself but do pay some attention to your pattern. Notice what physical reactions you have and what thoughts accompany them. Notice the variety of your body sensations, images, emotions, and thoughts. You may be surprised, so keep in mind you've been stuck in the same pattern for years—you just never noticed it before. If you can, take a look at the clock and see how long your reactions last. While it may not always be useful or productive to feel rage and fear, there isn't anything wrong or abnormal about it—it's what people do when they perceive a threat, even an imagined one. If you had perceived the threat that triggered your anger from a different perspective, would you have reacted in another way? Think about it.

It really is possible to be both a participant in a fight and an observer. We've tried it and so have the people we interviewed. The next time you're in the middle of a quarrel, pay close attention to the words each of you uses and notice your body language. (Remember how the quarrel started. Don't forget that an angry reaction is a response to some perceived threat.) As soon as you have achieved some distance, speculate (to yourself, not out loud) on what the perceived threat might have been. If you had been aware of his particular perspective, what would you have done? Would you have averted the fight or were you spoiling for one? Was one of you defending against a perceived but unintentional threat? What were you really arguing about?

When asked about the most common cause of arguments, people list a variety of subjects: money, perceived insults in front of others, how to handle the children, in-laws, how to spend free time and with whom, who cooks what, household responsibilities, how often to make love. Some people seem to enjoy arguing about everything, others not. Everybody can explain quite reasonably why any of these is a serious, real problem.

This is not to say that there aren't some very real problems that can be better solved with some outside help and counseling. However, in most relationships, many of the arguments are generated through misinterpretation—from the little voice in your head that has not really heard what the other person said. That voice plays a pre-recorded message which is likely to be your usual response to a perceived threat; it does not respond to reality.

*   *   *

Lisa described her fights with Hal. "They always start because he puts me down in front of other people."

"Are you sure that's what Hal's doing or is it the way you perceive it?" we asked her. We suggested she use her highly developed analytic skills to observe their next fight and let us know what happened.

"I was amazed," she told us a few weeks later. "I get angry so quickly that Hal doesn't even have a chance to finish a sentence. I just assume he's putting me down and fly into a rage. This time, I noticed how surprised he looked, and I began to wonder whether he means to put me down or if I hear it that way because I'm so afraid of being inadequate. I've worked in an industry where there are very few women. I've come to expect putdowns from men, so I'm always geared up to defend myself against them. I realized that the more unsure I'm feeling, the quicker I am to be offended. Poor Hal doesn't really have a chance no matter what he says."

Jenny's most frequent arguments with Ted are about disciplining the children. "He's much more strict than I am," she told us. "And I always rush to their defense. Then I feel guilty because I believe that we should be unified in dealing with the kids."

"What actually happens when you and Ted disagree?" we asked her.

She thought for a minute, then laughed. "I am immediately on the defensive. I assume he thinks I've done something wrong so I barely listen to him. As I think about it, I guess I believe if I did my job right, the kids would behave better. You know, maybe we aren't arguing about the kids at all. All our disagreements seem to occur when

I'm feeling uncertain about myself—not the kids—so I'm really just defending myself against my own guilt feelings. Amazing.''

Meg's and Josh's fights are about money. After our conversations, Meg told us she'd realized that she—not Josh—thought she was too extravagant. "The next time the subject came up, I didn't rush to defend myself. Instead, I watched his body language. He seemed worried, not angry, so I asked him about his work and the progress he's made on some specific problems he's been trying to resolve. And we didn't have a fight. I guess I've been arguing with myself about money, not Josh.''

There is a distinction between the facts that lead up to an argument and the experience of the argument. There is also a distinction between an event—happy or sad—and an individual experience of that event. When we are aware of those distinctions, we are in a position to choose suitable action.

Each of us is responsible for our own anger, which is not to say that people who are angry or resentful are "causing" their own anger. It is the difference between "I'm angry" and "You made me angry." In the former, we own the anger, in the latter, we've made someone else responsible for our emotional reactions. There is no real satisfaction in believing that someone else "causes" us to be angry or upset. Furthermore, being responsible for our own emotions doesn't mean that we are at fault. Most of us learned some time ago that there isn't any right or wrong about feelings—we just have them. Since all emotions are stimulated by our own perceptions, there *is* satisfaction and power in being responsible for them—if they are ours, we can change them. If they are someone else's, we are helpless because it is not easy to change someone else's behavior; it's not easy to change our own but at least we can be in control of ourselves.

Exploring our own perceptions by observing our own actions, making distinctions between facts and feelings, is enlightening and empowering. Making distinctions between our feelings and the facts of the event is also empowering, blaming other people is not. (Which is not to say that other people are right and we're wrong.) For example, spending time with a couple who drinks too much and becomes obnoxious produces some feelings in the couple who aren't drinking to excess. Most of us would choose not to spend time with the first couple, but that doesn't mean that one is "right" and the other "wrong." Spending a lifetime with a husband who is unloving, isn't caring or is abusive in some way also produces a variety of emotions. Most of us would choose not to live with that husband. But this book is about the cracks in a marriage and the disparities between expectations and reality, not the gaping holes. If you're in a marriage with gaping holes, seek outside counseling. It has been our experience that once you've achieved a shift in perception, you can demonstrate it by sharing your new awareness. In relationships filled with mutual caring, dramatic results occur from the sharing.

There is really no such thing as an argument-free relationship, and whether one would be preferable is open to question. Arguments do have positive value—they clear the air and allow us to clarify our feelings. And think of the good time you have when you make up.

Cleaning the Slate

Most love affairs begin with a clean slate—you don't know much about him, he doesn't know much about you. One of the hardest parts of creating a new love affair in an old marriage (when you are so familiar with each other) is cleaning the slate. Actually, you don't need a totally clean slate because you have shared a myriad of wonderful experiences and memories on which you can both draw to achieve this new perspective on your marriage. So, in this case, cleaning the slate means forgiving him and forgiving yourself for the various behaviors you don't like—yours and his. The same is true for him. Since it is hard to forgive anybody anything until you are sure what you like about them (if you don't know what you like about them, why bother to forgive them anything? In fact, why bother at all?), now is the time to remember what you like about him and what you like about yourself. When you feel comfortable with this process, share it with your husband.

Start by acknowledging your achievements so that you can derive satisfaction from them; don't leave out any success or accomplishment. Be thorough. Consider all your roles: wife, mother, daughter, career person, athlete, volunteer, pet owner, etc., and their responsibilities. Note how you fulfill these roles and whether you are acknowledged for the work you do. Did you plan to have a career? Do you have one? Have you had a positive impact on the people around you? Do you have children? Do you like them? Do you think you've done a good job? Did you decorate your home yourself? Are you pleased with it? Consider all the aspects of your life and your positive impact on them. (Now is not the time to assess your failures—besides, you probably do that all the time, anyway.)

When we asked Julie to tell us about all her achievements and satisfactions, she wasn't sure how to begin. "I've only been married for a year. I haven't done very much. After all, I'm only twenty-six."

"Didn't you just get a new job?" we asked her. "Tell us about it. Is it better than your last one?"

"As a matter of fact, it is. But I was so intent on leaving the old one and was so afraid that we wouldn't have enough money if I didn't get a new one fast, that I haven't really thought about how much better it is. I have a lot more responsibility now. The office is very high-pressure because we have some tremendously important deadlines, and I have to make sure that everyone else gets their jobs done. Come to think of it, I never thought I could handle a staff and have them like me—but they do! It's really nice." By this time Julie had begun to smile. "And my husband has been asking me to help him with his business. I never thought he'd do that—he always said I was too scatter-brained. I guess he knows I'm not. Maybe it's time I gave up that act."

"Can you think of anything else you like about yourself these days?"

"Well, yes, I guess I can. I like the way I'm getting along with my family. My parents have begun to ask my opinion on sticky family issues, and they seem to take my advice! They actually think I'm grown up. It feels real good."

"Anything else? Are you dressing differently?" we asked

"I guess I am. I look very professional when I go to work—not like a kid just out of college—and on weekends I'm not just in jeans anymore. I'm wearing some clothes that would have seemed too daring to put on before. I'm having a very good time."

In fact, Julie was quite pleased with herself, and she hadn't even noticed.

Laura is thirty-five, married for the second time, has a teenage son and two preteenage stepdaughters. We asked her the same questions. She also discovered she was pleased with her life but hadn't really noticed. Because she is always criticizing herself, she realized she never pats herself on the back.

"I've finally got the promotion I've been asking for—it's taken years, but I have it now! And I've decided to redecorate my office so that it reflects my title. Instead of being held up by red tape, I've figured out how to order the furniture so that there won't be any fuss."

"You realize," we pointed out to her, "that because you were finally willing to acknowledge your accomplishments, you were able to take the appropriate action—you cut through the red tape and no one minded because it was the right thing to do. Now, can you think of something at home that's changed because of your attention to it?"

"Yes. I've worked very hard to have a good relationship with my stepdaughters. I wanted them to know that I loved them, and I realized that a demonstration of my love had to include disciplining them when it was appropriate. I was very afraid to scold them during our first years together. But then I understood that we couldn't have any real communication without discipline. And, you know, we have a very good time together. We have a new family unit that we all enjoy."

"That's terrific. Is there anything else?"

"Yes, there is," Laura revealed. "I think it's time I dressed to reflect my age and my professional status. I've been thinking about how I want to look now, and I've decided that I don't want to hide anymore. I want clothes that will make a statement about how good I feel about myself. I'm ready to buy a whole new wardrobe."

Acknowledge Your Husband

Most of us don't take the time to notice the positive aspects of our lives. We take stock only when things appear to be going wrong or become unpleasant. Acknowledging your accomplishments will make a significant difference in how you feel about yourself, and your new positive self-image will affect how the people you love feel about you.

Now, do the same thing for your husband. Consider all his roles—husband, father, son, career person, athlete, volunteer, pet owner, etc.—and their responsibilities. Note how he fulfills these roles and whether he is acknowledged for the work he does. Does he acknowledge himself? What is his impact at work? Is he aware of his total impact or only a part of it? Does he assess it correctly? Is he satisfied with the way he spends his nonworking hours? Have you been listening to him? Or have you been feeling too resentful to hear him?

When Barry lost his job as an editor at a major newspaper, Beth was surprised to find she wasn't the least bit worried. In the four years they had been married, Barry had become clear about his career goals and he was comfortable with his responsibilities. Because he had shown confidence when he was employed, it was easy for Beth to be supportive and cheerful as they explored his options. Barry stayed confident. When he did find a new job, it was no surprise to Beth that it was much better than his previous one.

"Maybe I should tell him how terrific and competent I think he is. I'm not sure I ever really did that."

She did. The next evening Barry brought the subject up again, and she knew he wanted to hear it again. "So, I told him! He loved it," Beth reported to us.

Who Are You, Right Now?

Now that you're clear about what you like about yourself and your husband, you are closer to being able to forgive both of you for what it is about your relationship you *don't* like. Before you do, it's important to acknowledge how each of you has changed since your marriage. Who are you right now? Who is he?

Many of our ideas and attitudes about ourselves are leftovers from when we were much younger that continue to influence our decisions. They often show up in our current lives in very small ways, sometimes in such small ways that we don't notice them, just as we don't notice our anger. Nevertheless, these small ways make big statements about who we are and how we expect to be treated. Since they go unnoticed it is necessary to look for them in order to choose what is still appropriate and what is not, and to have a clean slate for your love affair with your husband. When Sue had her peak experience as she was cleaning out her closet, she noticed some of the decisions that were preventing her from being *who* she wanted to be, and from being treated *how* she wanted as well.

We asked Vivian what old decisions were still operative in her life and how she thought they were getting in her way. It took her some time to realize that, at forty-two, she had never worn a dark-colored lipstick because of something her father had said when she was fourteen. She was also convinced her husband did not like the way she looked anymore. She was amazed to discover that she had not changed her style of makeup since she was a teenager. She had decided she was allergic to lipstick (although she wasn't allergic to any other kind of makeup) because her father had embarrassed her by telling her she had fat lips. She'd made up the allergy in response to her husband's suggestion that she wear bright red lipstick. Clearly, the old decision prevented her from dressing in a style appropriate to the person she had become. Noticing the discrepancy was very liberating for Vivian, and she began the process of finding the right clothes and makeup for her. "We've had a great time," she told us. "My husband wants to go shopping with me now. He feels he's had an influence on how I look, and he's very pleased with himself. He's even decided that I look ten years younger these days! Who would have believed it?"

How have you developed and changed? How are you different right now? What about your husband? How is he different right now? How has he grown and changed? Think about how you would describe yourself and your husband to someone you haven't seen for a long time. What do you notice about yourself? What task have you recently completed that is a source of pleasure to you? Have you recognized your own accomplishments or are you simply waiting for someone else to acknowledge you? Now is the time to let yourself in on what everybody else in your life already knows. Once you've done that, you will be able to hear others acknowledge you. What small step can you take to acknowledge to yourself who and what you are right now? Do it.

Who Is He, Right Now?

Now, focus on feeling good about your husband. How has he changed since you got married? It will be much easier to answer the questions about him than it was to look at yourself. After all, for quite a while you have been watching, measuring, and gathering evidence about him—just waiting to be asked! But be fair. You began your self-research from an objective, outsider's point of view. So do the same for him. Imagine that you are describing someone else's husband and don't leave out anything good or special about him. (Remember this is not the time to list his faults. You do that often enough as it is.)

When she considered how her husband had changed since they got married, Leah realized that one of the biggest differences had to do with money. In their early years she thought Tim was stingy. Now, as she reviewed his role in the community, she realized that he had made significant contributions of his time, his talent as a lawyer, and his money to the causes that concerned them. She saw that it was no longer fair to view him as stingy; in fact, it probably never was. Rather, his way of dealing with money was a reflection of their limited resources and not his character. This new awareness allowed her to think about him in a new way. That night, Leah apologized to Tim for all the times she had been angry at him over the issue of money. And she told him how much she admired his professionalism and his participation in the community. "At first, Tim was startled," she reported. "But I could see he was real pleased that I'd bothered to tell him what I'd noticed. His grin started in his eyes and spread to his mouth. And then he gave me the warmest, biggest hug I can ever remember. It was all I needed. The champagne he brought home the next evening paled beside that wonderful hug."

What would your husband say if you asked him to describe how he is different from when you married him? What does he consider his most significant accomplishment? What does he really feel good about? Tell him what you have noticed. Ask him to tell you three things he would do exactly the same if he had them to do over. Ask him to tell you one thing he would have done differently and how. Ask him if he can forgive himself for what he did not know. Can you forgive him also?

Or is there some little resentment still lurking in the background? What joke do you wish he would stop telling? What friend do you wish he didn't see anymore? What ties does he keep wearing that you hate? What sweater should he throw out? Are you willing to let him eat butter pecan ice cream even if you hate it? Are you willing to accept him just the way he is? Good! Now you are ready to forgive him and yourself for being exactly the way you are. So forgive him, forgive yourself. Now, forgive each other.

Don't forget to tell him what you've discovered about each of you.

What to Do Now That You Know Who You Are

In our meetings with women, we discussed the way love affairs begin. Most agree that being in love sparks heightened feelings of physical attractiveness, well-being, and vitality. Some recall having a great deal more energy; others become aware of their bodies as if for the first time. All agree that love prompts them to do something to enhance their appearance—they feel they deserve it.

Ellen realized that before she's consciously aware of being in love, she is aware that she feels very good about herself—accomplished, powerful, organized, and cheerful. She recalls that she always loses weight, and she never diets intentionally.

Leslie gets ready to have an affair by choosing her clothes more carefully each morning. Instead of reaching into her closet and grabbing the first outfit, she chooses her image for the day. She takes more care with underwear and accessories to achieve her desired effect. During our discussions she was startled to realize that she always does this when she's met a new man.

Having a love affair means being excited, eager, cheerful, feeling fit, loving, lovable, and in full bloom. Women who are not married and looking for new relationships always do something special for themselves as they begin this process. They are usually not conscious of these actions. Since you are married and are not looking for a new man —only trying to see your man anew—you will have to make a conscious attempt to create for yourself the sense of well-being that single women describe. The action or feeling that is uniquely yours may be buried deep within you. Start thinking about doing things that make you feel good about yourself and do some of them.

Treat Yourself As If You Are Lovable

People only have love affairs when they feel lovable, and, in turn, can allow themselves to be loved. It's time to treat yourself as if you felt lovable. Do something special for yourself.

It could be something that you have put off or something of no interest to the rest of your family. It could be something you have not done for a long time because other things have taken precedence. It may be as simple as buying a new lipstick, finding an hour or two to get your hair cut, or having a professional manicure. Or would you love to choose an entirely different wardrobe? Would you like to go to the office wearing a teddy under your tailored navy suit? Would you like to start sleeping in a sexy black nightgown, silk pajamas, or even nothing at all? Have you been wearing Arpege or Miss Dior since you were nineteen? Are you ready to try Chloe or Joy? You may be pleased with your appearance but feel displeased with other aspects of your life. Are you longing to spend an hour browsing in a museum or a bookstore? Is there someone you've lost touch with whom you'd really like to see?

Whatever your action, it should stem from your acknowledgment of yourself as a lovable, worthwhile human being.

Do something similar for your husband. People who feel good about themselves are generous with other people. They are not afraid to offer sincere praise; they enjoy giving gifts—small and large; they make time to spend with others. Think about how you can express to your husband the love you feel for him. What big present would you buy him if you could? What small gift would demonstrate your affection? Has he always wanted you to watch a sports event with him? Have you ever agreed to do so cheerfully? Does he have a favorite dinner that you think is too fattening so you never make it? What gesture could you make that would tell him that you love him?

Suzanne decided to show her husband how much she cared for him by joining him in his den while he was watching a football game. "He knew that I was only there because I wanted to be near him. Neither of us said anything about how unusual it was for me to sit through something I consider a huge bore. We didn't have to talk about it, though. I knew he knew—he was massaging my feet the entire time. That's my favorite thing and I know he's not crazy about doing it."

How lovable do you both feel now?

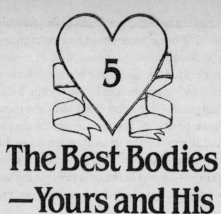

The Best Bodies
—Yours and His

He always tells you how beautiful, desirable, smart, and sexy you are. He always does something special. In a crowded room, even in the midst of an important conversation, his eyes find you, and he manages a lustful yet gentle and appealing glance. His body fits yours perfectly, on the dance floor and in bed. Your sexual appetites are well matched. You are wild about every inch of his body—the hair curling around his ears, the hollows of his neck, the curve of his buttocks, the hair on his chest, the ripple of his thigh muscles. His love making starts languidly with long, lingering kisses over every inch of your body and culminates in exquisite, deep penetration. Another time he is ribald and zesty, hugging, licking, and kissing you to a passionate lust that climaxes with you riding him high into oblivion. You have been known to leave parties to make love on the beach or even on your own comfortable bed.

He loves to sleep entwined with you, calling attention to the contrast between his long leanness and your soft curves and how well you fit. He always invites you into the shower and can be counted on to find something new and terrific about your body—and he never fails to tell you.

Is that a perfect description of you and your husband? Or could you disagree with all or most of it? In fact, you hardly make love anymore—certainly you don't take showers together. You can't remember the last time he complimented your body or you told him you like his. When you get right down to it, you don't like his body much these days, and you definitely don't like your own. Or you may still like his and hate yours. Or you may feel fine about both but you're dissatisfied with how they're relating. The idea for a love affair may begin in the mind, but there is simply no way to have it without your current physical equipment. You can tell how you are feeling about yours by considering the following:

Do you:

1. Undress only in the bathroom?
2. Partially undress in front of him, then quickly put on your nightgown to make sure you aren't naked while the lights are on?
3. Never consider joining a health club because there is no place to undress in private?
4. Never allow yourself to dream of having a love affair with a stranger because you would have to take your clothes off with the lights on?

61

5. Still have all the clothes you ever bought that you loved and can't wear because you are now too fat or too thin?

6. Buy a lot of shoes but not too many dresses, skirts, and certainly no pants?

7. Feel that buying a bathing suit requires a battle plan suitable for a major Marine operation?

8. Have rules about clothes? Nothing sleeveless, nothing too chic, no bright colors, no prints. You buy only classics because you expect to wear them for many years.

9. Move quickly away when anyone holds a loaded camera in your direction?

10. Hate to look at your wedding pictures?

If any of the above is true for you, and you don't like what has happened to your body or to his over the years, you have a problem. There are some obvious solutions, and we'd never suggest they aren't worth pursuing. People have experienced great satisfaction in getting their bodies back into shape by dieting or working out, and some even have body surgery. The decision to try one of these remedies is frequently appropriate and always personal. Unfortunately, none produce results overnight, so since you're planning a love affair right now, a diet or even some stronger measure won't make any difference—you can't wait till you feel (or look) thinner or fatter.

"Why not?" you ask. "I can put off this love affair until I think I look better. I mean, I've waited this long, why not a little longer? Especially if I'm going to begin a program to pull myself together. He's not going anywhere, is he?"

Is he? Could he? And why wait to find out when all you have to do is discover something about yourself that you value? That's all it will take to begin feeling good enough —and sexy enough—about your body to risk displaying it in a daring way. Since you are married to this man, is it really such a big risk to take?

Consider how insecure most people are about their body image. Have you ever known anyone who actually thought he or she had a great body? Even the people we admire most for their physical attributes tend to feel just as inadequate as the rest of us. If you don't believe us, talk to someone you know whom you consider physically fit and sexy. Compliment them on some physical attribute you admire. We guarantee that they'll say, "Thanks. But I really hate my nose. It's too long (short, crooked, etc.)." In their heart of hearts, they don't like their bodies any more than you like yours. They have a difficult time experiencing how good they look. Thin adults who were fat kids have a hard time remembering that they're not fat anymore. Our negative body images (whether real or imagined) invariably interfere with an accurate appraisal of ourselves.

It's worth the effort, right now, to tell yourself some objective truths about your body and to find something you like about it. For those of you who feel good about your body, reassessing it will only serve to heighten your good feelings.

The next time you are about to take a bath or shower, stand in front of a full-length mirror without any clothes on. Take a good, long look at yourself and describe what you see without using any negatives. Don't lie, but do tell the truth in a positive way. For example, instead of saying, "My hair is too thin and drab," say, "My hair is soft and fine, with gold highlights." When you have described your entire body, notice the features you found very attractive and describe them in concrete words so there is no mistaking what you mean. For example, instead of saying, "I like my skin," say, "I like the color of my skin. I like how soft and smooth it feels, especially on the backs of my hands, on my stomach, and on my thighs."

Maureen did this exercise at a body-awareness seminar. Her first reaction was embarrassment—she didn't want to see her body at all. She realized she'd always made sure that she never really looked at herself in mirrors—she used them to put on makeup, comb her hair, check her hemlines, and she was always as perfunctory as possible so she wouldn't actually see herself. It wasn't that she thought she was too fat or too thin, too short or too tall; she just didn't like her body very much. Since she was in a group and everyone was standing in front of mirrors, Maureen couldn't avoid looking at herself. So she did. It didn't take her very long to notice that there was nothing wrong with her body at all. In fact, now that she was finally really seeing it, she realized it was a good body—she even rather liked it. Her relief was so great that she laughed out loud!

You may not be as lucky as Maureen, but there is no question that you will find something that you do like about yourself—your hair or your eyes, your hands or the shape of your feet, the color of your skin, the curve of your hip, or the length of your legs. When you discover it, say it out loud. Tell yourself what you like. Pay yourself a compliment. Really hear it.

Hearing a compliment almost always produces a smile and a sense of well-being, however fleeting. Since your goal is to achieve a greater sense of well-being so that you'll be willing to take risks, practice giving yourself compliments. Say them out loud when you're alone. Do it even if you feel silly. At the same time, allow yourself to hear the nice things other people say to you. The better you feel about yourself, the easier it is to feel sexy. (More about the importance of compliments in Chapter 6.)

We all know certain women who seem to catch every male (as well as female) eye when they enter a room. These women are often not the most beautiful or even the best dressed, yet they seem the most attractive. What these women have in common is their sense of self-worth; they are confident and sure of themselves and, as a result, project an irresistible vibrancy and vitality. All of us have had moments we remember as particularly successful. They've usually occurred when we felt accomplished and worthwhile, when our self-esteem was at a high. Then we felt irresistible, too. And we were.

Joanne remembers the evening she went to an industry cocktail party with her husband and saw a lot of people she hadn't seen for some time. The previous six months had been very gratifying for her: she'd started her own business that was well on its way to being a success. Though she had gained some weight and was self-conscious about her appearance, she did feel good and was looking forward to sharing her accomplishment with her industry colleagues.

As soon as she entered the room, people came up to greet her. "I felt like a million dollars," she told us. "Even though I was barely paying my bills, I just felt so good about myself that I seemed to be irresistible. That's what my husband told me later that night. Actually, he's been telling me what great shape he thinks I'm in and has never commented on the weight I've gained. I'm the one who seems to mind. But I didn't the night of that party!"

Can you remember the last time you felt that way yourself? Where were you? What were you doing? What had produced your self-confidence? Did anyone notice or say anything? Did you do anything about it? Allow yourself to remember and experience that good feeling.

Feeling Fit As Well As Sexy

Feeling fit and sexy definitely starts with one's own experience and not someone else's opinion. We may need feedback from others for reinforcement, but we won't hear it until we begin to feel it ourselves. And feeling it has very little to do with some objective evaluation of how we look. Taking opportunities to notice your own body and finding ways to compliment yourself is the best way to begin. What do you do that makes you feel that you look good?

"I love to dance. I may feel fat and flabby before I go out, but afterward, I always feel that my body is terrific," Tina revealed. "So I will jump at any opportunity to go dancing. Frequently, it's the only exercise I do, and I'm willing to be uncomfortable the next day since I don't do it often enough to get all my muscles in shape. And you know what? I'm not even embarrassed to admit that I'm a great dancer—how could I not be when it makes me feel so good?"

Janet told us that she had spent a week at tennis camp with her husband. "For the first few days I felt inept. I was exhausted, and when I crawled into bed at night I sure didn't want to make love. I hated my husband for making me go and myself for agreeing. In the middle of the week, I started to notice an improvement in the way I was hitting the ball. After that, I could hardly wait to get back to the courts for more. I felt that my body was terrific, that I could control it, and I wanted to use it in every way I could. Then I noticed that I couldn't keep my hands off him. Boy, was he pleased!''

Most of us only notice our bodies when something is wrong—and we notice because we aren't feeling very good about ourselves in the first place. This is true whether we are feeling fat and flabby, thin and stringy, or just plain sick. There is certainly medical evidence suggesting that when we are not feeling good about our lives, when we are feeling tense and anxious, we are more prone to illness. On the other hand, once we've decided to diet or eat more or see a doctor, we have begun to pay our bodies the positive attention that, in turn, promotes a feeling of well-being. As a first step to feeling fit and sexy, engage in any of the physical activities that strengthen and flex the muscles. If you're not athletic, try walking purposefully for some period of time every day. For the more athletically inclined, jogging, skiing, playing tennis, swimming, or an exercise routine should be added to your schedule. Exercise increases our self-esteem, almost as if our bodies are returning the favor.

Even without exercising or working out, you can increase your positive awareness of your own body by noticing what you like about it. Joanne liked her body more when she felt good about her work; Tina liked the way her body moved when she danced; Janet liked the way her body responded when she pushed it at tennis camp. What do you like about your body? Find out. And when you do, don't let yourself forget it!

How Do You Feel About Your Husband's Body?

Finding out how you feel about your husband's body presents no problem. You already know what you think of it, and since you are planning to have a love affair with him, its shape, size, good and bad features, cannot be all that important; it's clearly not an issue. Aren't you pleased to be finished with that conversation?

How he feels about his body may present another problem. A man who is overweight, underexercised, or generally dissatisfied with his appearance may not wish to use his body in a fully loving way. (Men are really no different from women in this—something most women tend to forget.) And since he is no more likely than you to go on a diet just because somebody else suggested it, your only approach is to appreciate his body just the way it is.

You can begin by giving him small gifts. A long-handled loofah he can use in the shower or bath, a fragrant new aftershave, silk briefs or a new pair of boxer shorts made of the finest Egyptian cotton—just about anything that feels good on his skin and lets him know you're thinking of his body.

Massage As Message

Another even more delightful way to express appreciation for another's body is massage. Giving your husband an all-over body massage is a lovely and loving gift to his body. It may even inspire him to return the favor. You can do it with the lights on or off. It can be merely a sensuous experience, or the beginning of a wonderful, sexy night. You don't have to take a course in massage (though that might be fun too). If you are timid about starting with an all-over body massage, begin by rubbing only the back of his neck and shoulders. Do it wherever he happens to be sitting. Where you massage his body, how much and when, is not important—what *is* important is the attention you are paying him.

As you rub, notice the line of muscles along his shoulders. Ask him if it feels good and if he would like you to exert more pressure. Ask him if he would like you to move down his back and if he would like to have more of his body massaged. You don't have to do it then. You can make a date for later. You don't even have to ask him any questions. The point is to get started in any way that is comfortable for you.

When you are ready to do an all-over massage, make sure you have the right supplies at hand. They can be as simple or elaborate as you choose. You can begin with whatever is already in your medicine cabinet or cosmetic case. Put a few drops of baby oil in your palms; this will ensure that the rubbing will be smooth and sensual, not abrasive. Or you can go to one of the shops specializing in beauty supplies and stock up on unguents and ointments.

The best way to learn more about massage techniques is to have one yourself. The second best way is to read books about it. (Of course, if you're only reading about massage, you will have greater difficulty imagining how it would feel.) From both these sources you will learn what you like and what you don't. This may not be exactly the same for him, but the only way to find that out is to try it. Nevertheless, once you have had your own massage, you'll realize what a sensuous experience it is and how relaxing it can be.

Most of all, you'll understand how it would be even better if the masseuse/masseur were someone you loved.

Trained masseuses/masseurs each have special techniques. Their goal is to relax your body, not to caress you, but you can adapt their techniques to do both. There are rules for each type of massage, which needn't concern you unless you choose to become an expert. The purpose of your massage is to become expert at having a love affair with your husband.

As you move over each part of his body during your massage, call his attention to what you are doing. As you talk about the parts of his body you particularly like, it may surprise him but he will start to notice how good it feels to be touched, and it will be hard for him not to like it. He will, in fact, begin to realize what he likes about his body. Tell him how you always notice his forearms when his shirt sleeves are rolled up or how the muscles in his back ripple when he moves in a certain way. Does he have a terrific backside? Tell him. Tell him what it is about his body that turns you on. If you feel embarrassed, do it anyway—because you have nothing to lose by telling him and a lot more to lose if you don't. Take the risk. Remember, compliments always cause a sense of well-being, and that's exactly what you want to give your husband. So, what is it that you like about his body? Tell him.

Once you have gone as far as giving him a massage, you will be ready to learn more about what turns you on. If you already know, congratulations! Start letting him know so the two of you can have fun together. (And you can skip ahead to the next chapter.) If you're not sure or are having difficulty communicating what you need and want, congratulations! You're embarrassed like the rest of us, so read on.

The Purring Pussycat—Getting Him To Give You A Massage

Do you know what turns you on? What do you do with your knowledge? We've talked to many women and, unanimously, they say they like to be stroked. Constance told us that she thinks women are like pussycats who, when stroked, start to purr. "You know that low-pitched, throaty sound cats make when they deign to be petted? Did you ever notice what a cat does when she wants stroking? She moves close, sits on laps, climbs on bosoms, finds ways to place her body under a hand."

When women want stroking, we are not usually so direct. Many of us ask for it in such negative ways—by getting irritable, acting neglected or misunderstood—that we usually fail. No one voluntarily strokes a spitting cat; only a purring pussycat gets what she wants.

The option is clear: deign to be stroked. Climb into laps. Find soft places to nuzzle—and purr.

If you have not been paying much attention to what turns you on or, for that matter, haven't allowed yourself to be turned on at all recently, you need to rediscover your own purring pussycat. This is simple to do.

Sensual pleasure is an all-over feeling. It is enhanced by the feel of soft fabrics next to the skin, by pleasant scents emanating from clothing, by the glow of well-being. Sexual pleasure cannot be achieved unless you appreciate your own body. Most of us spend so much time and energy trying to change our bodies that we give little attention to what is good about them. We are all sexual beings with specific desires. While these feelings may be buried, they remain close to the surface. You can access them anytime, anywhere. You can begin on your way to work or to pick up the kids, in the supermarket or in the shower, or while you are cooking dinner. Allow yourself to notice how your clothes feel against your body. Notice how your legs feel when you're walking. How long is your stride? How does it feel? How do your hips move? Do you let your arms swing freely or are you always carrying things and never have them free? Notice that. Take a complete inventory of your entire body and how it feels when you move. You may find places that ache. You may decide to start an exercise program. You will also find things that you like. Once you do, it's difficult not to feel like having that part of your body stroked, caressed, hugged—and then loved.

The best way to rediscover what turns you on is to notice it when you are making love. Try to become aware of this the next time you and your husband are having sex. (You might even initiate it as soon as possible to get the information immediately.) You are absolutely not allowed to focus on what he does that you *don't* like—pay attention only to what you *do* like. For instance, you hate it when he sticks his tongue in your ear, but you love the way he wraps his arms around you because it makes you feel small and delicate. Pay no attention to the tongue (or move your head). Pay lots of attention to being hugged. What else does he do that you like? What doesn't he do that you would like? How can you get him to do more of that?

Have the courage to admit what you like to your husband. He'd probably be pleased to do it if only you'd ask. If you're not used to discussing this sort of thing, now is the time to take the risk. If you begin by telling him what you do like, he will feel complimented (remember, compliments are hard to resist), and he'll want to do more to please you.

If you're not sure you can experiment while you're making love, start your discovery in the same way you got him to notice his body. Ask him to give you a massage. (You can begin by asking him to rub your neck, and then . . . you know the rest.)

There are supposedly endless positions in which to make love. This book neither reviews them nor includes any information on them. We believe there probably are endless variations and urge you to create your own program of discovery. We are more interested in the apparently endless attitudes and emotions one can experience before, during, and after sexual activity. Here are some:

1. I am turned on and need a fix.
2. He is turned on and needs a fix.
3. We are turned on and need a fix.
4. God, I love him. I gotta get my hands on him.
5. Isn't this fun?
6. What can I do to make this last forever?
7. What could I do to get him into bed, right now?
8. He looks good enough to eat!
9. How would it feel if he bit me right here?
10. Where are his sweet spots?
11. Well, I don't have anything else to do right now.
12. I wonder what it would be like with Robert Redford?
13. Well, it's good exercise.
14. If I don't stop him, it will be over soon.
15. Oh God, isn't it over yet?
16. He didn't brush his teeth, and he drank too much.
17. How come he can't find my sweet spots?
18. I have a headache.
19. I wish I could go to sleep.

Now that you know what turns you on (and you've told your husband) and you've been having a great time, what do you do when you're truly not in the mood but you don't want to hurt his feelings?

When You're Not in the Mood

How do you know you're not in the mood? Does some little voice pipe up in your head: "Not now, I love this book!" or "I'm too tired," or "It tickles." Or does it say: "He ate garlic for supper!" What do you do when that happens? Are you able to say "no" so pleasantly that your husband never minds? Or do you create tension between you when you're not willing to make love? For that matter, how do you behave when you want to and he doesn't?

Does the voice in your head really know whether or not you're in the mood? How does it know? Does it know how to help you play tennis, ski, or golf? Or does it get in the way and make it hard for you to play well? Does it help you walk down the street? Or can you do that without it telling you how to walk? Does it know how to spend money? Is it good at it? Or does it sometimes tell you to buy the wrong thing? What does that voice in your head say when you're on a diet? Doesn't it always want ice cream or chocolate when you swore you wouldn't eat any? Does it tell you to wear nice clean underwear in case you're in an accident, and whose voice is that? Yours or your mother's? What does that voice know about your body? Does it tell you how to make love? Can you make love with that voice in your head? Do you always listen to it?

What does the voice in your head (Tim Gallwey calls it "Self 1"; others call it the mind) know about making love?

Was it there the last time you had an orgasm? Did it tell you how to have one? Or was it enjoying what you were doing too much to interfere? What has your mind ever done regarding your sex life other than try to turn you off? Your mind can be counted on to do the taxes and analyze investments, to choose the right schools for your children, to decide the best place to spend your winter or summer vacation, and to make sure you don't have an orgasm. It may have kept you out of trouble in the backseat of cars when you were in high school; it may help you keep your mouth shut when a snappy retort to your mother-in-law or your boss is particularly tempting, but it can't do you any good at all in bed. So forget it! Laugh at it! Make a date with it for later. It is trying to control your body's reactions at a time when you should tell it to buzz off.

"Not so easy to do," you say. "Easier than you think," we answer. If you can resist saying the wrong thing to your mother-in-law or your boss, you can resist saying "no" to your husband. You actually have more to lose by *not* resisting that negative voice when it comes to making love with your husband. And you do want to have an affair with him before someone else does, don't you? In fact, you may not know how to get yourself in the mood. When we realized that we didn't know what happens in the body and brain when we are in love and what causes us to be sexually aroused, we did some reading to find out. What we discovered may help you to understand how to get yourself in the mood. Arousal begins in the limbic system. (See *The Body Book* by David Bodonis.) Through two neurotransmitters, substances called "neopinephrine" and "dopamine" are released. These are similar to amphetamines but are produced naturally. These amphetaminelike substances are responsible for the "turned on" sensation we all treasure.

This process can be triggered by memory. It is why reading erotic passages turns us on and why hearing certain music makes us feel sexy. The words and music speak to memories of our own past sensual experiences. And we get turned on again.

Scientists know that the brain triggers physical sensations. It is possible to stimulate the brain to send out the "sexy" signal to your body. Often, we don't allow ourselves to do that; we get in our own way. Instead of allowing ourselves to be turned on, we think we should be doing the dishes or the work we brought home from the office or walking the dog. Starting the process is surprisingly easy. Simply evoke the experiences you associate with being turned on—by remembering and visualizing them.

While writing this book, both of us evoked old memories and each got turned on and felt sexy. Frequently this occurred when Sue's husband was out of town or Alice was away from her lover. Because it was so easy to turn ourselves on when we're alone, each made a point of trying it "in company." And it worked!

When your husband wants to make love and you don't, remember—you can turn yourself on if you choose to. Remind yourself that you love him and that you like being close to him. Remember the parts of your body you most like to have stroked and rubbed. Put his hand there. Remind yourself that the voice that says "no" is not an expert on what's good for you. Don't give your husband any excuses. Instead, tell the voice in your head that you'll speak with it later, and go ahead—make love.

We are not advocating a passive acceptance of "he's the man, he's right even when he's wrong!", nor do we mean to suggest that wives have to deliver sexually no matter what. We are making another distinction here between facts and feelings, or, in this case, facts and the thought "I'm not in the mood." Since, as most of us know, we don't act on every thought we have, we're suggesting that, from time to time, this is a thought that could be ignored.

Of course, there may be times when it isn't the voice in your head that's in the way; you may not feel well or you may have a deadline or one of the kids is sick. In that case, make it clear that you wish you were up to it or could delay your work. Sometimes getting in the mood just isn't possible. So instead of being annoyed or defensive, start to observe exactly what you do when the two of you are out of sync. Notice if you ever tell him why you're not in the mood. Notice if you're able to use humor. You could say, "I'll be right there—as soon as I finish taking Timmy's temperature, changing his diapers and his sheets, so start without me!" Or you could try simple affection and say, "Let's just hold each other tight." Whatever you do, don't get angry at his gesture of love or lust (if that's all you think it is just at that moment). Make a date for later and ask him to tell you what he'll do then.

Does it ever seem like more trouble than its worth? Is it? Could you imagine telling him how to improve his lovemaking so that you wouldn't feel that way? Could you? The point is to examine closely the reason you want to say no to discover if you can change your response.

"I really decided to give it a try," Linda told us. "The next time my husband wanted to have sex and the thought occurred to me that I wasn't in the mood, I just ignored it. I wanted to see what would happen. I was astounded at how quickly the thought went away, and I was very much in the mood. It was actually a liberating experience to realize that the thought didn't have to be true. Since then it's been pretty easy not to give any thought to the thought. I just let it go away and have fun."

If you want to make love and your husband doesn't, don't get angry with him. Instead, just give him a kiss or a quick hug and let it go for now. Again, suggest that the two of you just hold each other. Chances are that the closeness will appeal to him as much as it does to you and you both may be surprised. In any event, it is important to allow your husband the freedom to say "no," too, without it becoming a problem.

In either case, if you are both saying no to each other more often than yes, perhaps some counseling is in order.

Hopefully, you now know some things about yourself—and your marriage—you didn't before. Isn't it time to recast yourself in a new role in your own life?

Do You Look the Part?

Every time you get dressed to go out for the evening, you feel sexy and delicious. You know that your clothes are a perfect reflection of who you are so you are free to choose anything from your closet and know you'll feel and look good.

Every time you walk into a roomful of people, heads turn in your direction, people comment on how wonderful you look. You receive compliments graciously because you feel so at ease with yourself that other people's acknowledgment always makes you feel wonderful, never embarrassed.

Every time you see your friends, they tell you how much they admire your style. When your husband sees you, you can tell by the look in his eyes that he thinks you are a turned-on, sexy lady, and he'd do anything in the world for you. But first, he'd like to take you in his arms and ravish you.

* * *

Is that how it is for you? Or are you more likely to feel uncomfortable and uncertain about your appearance? You're not always sure you know what styles are right for you; in fact, often you get dressed as quickly as you can so you won't have to spend too much time worrying about what to wear or how you look. Whenever you receive a compliment, you change the subject. And really, you have no idea what your husband thinks about the way you look these days because he never comments, and you wouldn't dream of asking him. You'd like to do something about it, but it seems like a monumental task. You're not sure what to do, so you've convinced yourself that you really don't have the time anyway.

You are not alone; many women feel this way. Unless someone has persuaded you to take a course or read a book on dressing for success, you're like the rest of us: you have a few outfits in which you feel smashing. Otherwise, you're making do with what you've got, and you put "buy new clothes" and "clean out closets" on a "to do" list you might get to sometime in the next five years.

It is not uncommon for women of all ages—from twenty-five to seventy-five—to have an inaccurate picture of themselves. As Sue's mother says, "I'm always startled by what I look like. I don't feel like I'm over seventy; I feel twenty-five. I see myself and I think, 'Could that be me?'"

Old Pictures—New Looks

Most of us are shocked to discover that we look different than we feel. Because there is such a difference between our reality and our perception, we have only a vague idea of what image we're projecting. And we rarely know with any accuracy how other people see us. In our mind's eye is the image of ourselves that we developed in high school or college or the night we became engaged or the day we got married, and we have formed no new pictures since. The last time you looked at old photographs of yourself, did you wonder what has happened to that young vibrant person? Did you think you looked eager, open, smooth-skinned, and pretty? Do you think you look that way now? Do you think you look older than you are? (You probably think you have too many wrinkles, but then so does everybody.) Do you have an accurate perception of how old you do look? It's confusing, and certainly easier not to think about it. But slipping into familiar clothes and familiar patterns keeps us stuck in old routines, old points of view, and leaves no room for new possibilities. If you're carrying around old images of how you look and every time you catch a glimpse of yourself you're disappointed or surprised, your self-esteem is likely to be low. It's definitely time to take some new pictures and see yourself as you really are—not compared to what you used to look like, not compared to anyone.

When we first fall in love, we take special care with our clothes; we pamper our bodies. We don't do this consciously—we seem to know instinctively that how we look makes a statement about how we feel. When we feel good about ourselves, we are luminescent: we stand straight and smile a lot. Being in love enhances our self-esteem. We feel worthy and look and act accordingly. This sense of worthiness is empowering but frequently misinterpreted. Instead of realizing that it is self-generated we attribute it to someone else. People tell us, "You look wonderful. You must be in love." We blush and smile and forget the time we spent on ourselves. Yet any action that enhances our well-being increases our self-esteem. This includes changing our hairdo, getting a manicure, taking exercise classes, or stopping smoking. When we increase our self-esteem, we expect to be loved and send out signals accordingly. When we feel depressed, unhappy, overworked, overweight, and overwhelmed, our body language, including the clothes we choose, signals that as well. If you don't like the way you look, whether consciously or not, how lovable do you think you are?

In order to have a love affair with your husband before someone else does, you have to start feeling lovable and you have to look the part—for you and for him. You need to provide tangible, visible clues to the profound changes you are making. If you have buried your sexy, sensuous self so deeply that you are barely aware of it, your husband would have to be a CIA operative to decipher how you feel inside.

"If he really cared about me," you say, "he'd know immediately that I have a different attitude about our marriage." Indeed, it's all too easy to come up with a lot of reasons why it's unnecessary to update your appearance:

1. I'm too busy—full-time job, kids, cooking, cleaning, car pooling, etc.
2. Being a mother isn't sexy.
3. I'm not the frilly type.
4. My husband loves me just the way I am.
5. I'm too tired.
6. Nothing I do will make any difference.
7. I'm on a tight budget.
8. Being a wife is not a sexy job. Besides, I don't want to look sexy, I just want to feel sexy.
9. My husband doesn't notice my clothes so why bother?

* * *

We could go on, but since you've probably added your own excuses, there's no need. However, if your husband truly doesn't pay attention to how you look, there's a chance he's making love to you with the lights off or in some other perfunctory fashion, and it's time to change all that. You don't have to dress as if you're constantly about to stage a big seduction scene. You do have to enhance your best features in a feminine, up-to-date style appropriate to who you are, what's important to you now, and *not* representative of your old ideas and attitudes.

But you can't make appropriate changes in your appearance until you have a clear picture of what you look like. We all know women who were beautiful brides, who two, five, or ten years later are unrecognizable as the beauties they once were. Chances are, they've given up on themselves; certainly, they don't have a clear idea of what they look like anymore.

Robin had always looked younger than she was. "When I was in my mid-twenties, I hated looking eighteen, and I did everything I could to make myself look older. Of course, by the time I was thirty-five, I loved the fact that no one could tell my age, and I encouraged this deception by letting my hair grow down the middle of my back. And I was still putting on makeup the way I did when I first learned how at thirteen. I thought I'd pulled it off brilliantly, and in some ways I had. But the truth is I was not dressing in a way appropriate to the woman I had become, and I didn't feel very comfortable with myself. When I saw myself on a TV talk show, I was dismayed: my face looked old and harsh, framed by much too much hair. I looked so much older than my mental picture. I felt very confused, and had no idea what to do about it.

"Then one of my friends suggested I go to a professional to show me how to use makeup in a different way. And I had my hair cut. At first, I felt like the same old me. But I knew I had a new look. Still, I felt resigned to looking like a forty-year-old—whatever that looks like. Secretly, I was pleased. It was a relief to tell the truth about my age. The biggest surprise was my friends' reactions—they all thought I looked ten years younger and wanted to know what I'd done! Suddenly, I realized that dressing inappropriately had actually made me look older, not younger."

If we make decisions about our clothes, makeup, and hairstyles based on inaccurate mental pictures, we make mistakes, we don't look our best, and we rob ourselves of the pleasure and satisfaction that accompany knowing and liking who we are. And many women have not changed their style since they were teenagers. (Some women, of course, are right on target and know that an ongoing assessment keeps them up to date.)

How we present ourselves also affects how people react to us. The most effective way to change others' attitudes to us (you can't simply tell someone how to behave toward you) is to change ourselves. This illustrates a crucial cycle: our beliefs influence our own perceptions; our perceptions are reflected in our actions; then our actions—our behavior, manners, and dress—influence other peoples' perceptions of us. The key to creative change is in examining the unconscious belief that determines our self-perception.

Underlying Robin's style of dress was her unconscious belief that she would somehow escape the aging process. The actions she took (how she chose her clothes, makeup, and hairstyle) reinforced that belief. These influenced other people's perceptions of her, unfortunately not exactly as she intended. Because her physical appearance did not reflect her accomplishments, she did not advance professionally as far as she might have. And she was fooling no one about her age but herself.

In a workshop on self-presentation, Melanie had an opportunity to reconsider what statement she was making about herself, what people saw when they met her, and how they reacted to her. She describes the shock she felt when she saw herself on videotape. "For the taping, I had to introduce myself and tell where I lived, what work I do, that sort of thing, none of which was embarrassing or difficult. I don't mind telling how long I've been married—in fact, I'm rather proud of it. But I was very nervous in front of the camera. Nevertheless, I thought I'd covered it up and delivered my lines with my usual openness. I was dressed informally, my hair was combed as usual—pulled back in a bun. Later, when we were all watching the tapes we'd made, I was shocked and surprised to see how formal and severe I looked—and how unfriendly. I certainly didn't look as sexy as I feel. My appearance seemed the opposite of how I felt. Other people commented on my stiffness and my formidable stance. No one saw me as outgoing or friendly.

"I was really stung by their words—so different from the way I describe myself. And I began to wonder what my husband thought of me after so many years of marriage. I realized that we had lost much of our spontaneity.

"As a result of the videotape experience, I decided it was time to make some changes. First, I got a haircut; then, I picked out new colors for makeup and my basic wardrobe. When I attended a reunion of the people in my workshop, they all commented on how much more attractive I looked.

They used words like open, friendly, and accessible to describe my appearance. I was delighted by my success. So was my husband. 'If it's a workshop that did it, go to as many as you want,' he told me. Now I take great care with what I wear so that people will know who I am. I don't want to hide it ever again."

It may be as difficult to change our ideas about ourselves as it is to change others' ideas about us. We're all expert at supporting (and reinforcing) our points of view—most of us can go on for hours describing what motivates a particular pattern of behavior. Some of us are so good at this that no one even attempts to show us a new way of viewing an old problem. Mainly, we don't notice our inconsistencies until we are shocked, somehow, into recognition. Until Robin saw herself on the TV talk show, she had collected a lot of evidence proving that if she kept her hair long and wore the same makeup she wore as a teenager, no one would ever guess how old she really was. Afterward, she understood how wrong her assessment had been.

When we make new decisions that lead to action, we do not always feel comfortable, and this discomfort stops many people before they start. Perhaps Melanie would not have enrolled in her workshop if she'd known ahead of time how uncomfortable she would feel. Yet, it did produce some dramatic changes in her, and as we have seen, she is delighted.

To begin the process of change, we must first find a way to see ourselves clearly—to know what we really look like. Not everyone has access to videotape; everyone does have access to their image in a mirror. Find some way to sneak up on yourself—catch yourself in a store window or an oversize department store mirror. Create the element of surprise for yourself. You may think this sounds silly; however, most of us have difficulty staring at ourselves—even if there's nobody else around—and more often than not, what we see is our mental picture and not the real person.

Your goal now is to achieve the most objective view possible—see yourself as if you were an observer. Who is the person you're looking at? Old? Young? Fat? Thin? Dowdy? Matronly? Sprightly? Cheerful? Sad? Attractive? Pathetic? Notice what your clothes, makeup, and haircut say about you. Notice any inconsistencies in how you dress and who you are now. Are you a successful career woman who looks like a dumpy housefrau? Are you a young mother dressed as if you're an executive? Are your kids in college, while you look like you're about to go on a sixties peace march? Have you been wearing that pleated skirt for so many years it's back in style? Describe that person reflected in the glass. Does that description reflect how you feel about yourself? Is it better or worse than you thought? Do you think you look as good as you feel? If you don't feel good about yourself, is it reflected in your appearance or do you think you've hidden it successfully? Do you look like someone who is having a love affair with her husband?

Closet Revelations

Armed with an accurate idea of how you look in your clothes, you can evaluate the coded signals they are sending. Are they the messages you want to send? If you think you look sexy and no one seems to notice, you are sending a garbled message. If you don't want to look sexy, ask yourself why. Either way it's time to take some drastic steps. It's time to clean out your closet. Yes, it's time to move that chore to the top of the "to do" list and get it done. And, like all chores we put off, once begun it creates its own momentum. You might even enjoy it and the benefits are obvious: you'll feel virtuous, you'll be taking an action that demonstrates your new decisions about yourself, you'll have room for new things if you choose to buy any, and when you're finished, you'll know that everything you own fits not just you but who you are.

Carole Jackson, in *Color Me Beautiful,* describes one approach to this process. Ours is slightly different. For this exercise, follow these rules: give away, throw out, or store (if you have the space) every outdated item of clothing: too tight or too loose, frayed or worn, out of style, or one you hate. If your husband hates something, get rid of it. Especially get rid of anything that makes you feel like a martyr. You know, the dress that cost a fortune and has never fit but since you're not a billionaire, you *have* to keep wearing it. Do not keep anything because you don't have the money to replace it. Chances are you won't need to—you have more clothes than you think. Keep only those clothes that make you feel attractive.

As you touch each item, tell yourself why you have kept it. By becoming aware of the stories attached to items of clothing, you will discover some old decisions you've made about yourself. These can be given away along with the clothes to make room for new ones. Oddly enough, creating order and making space in our physical world creates order and openness in our emotional lives. It makes room for new possibilities.

Kate discovered that she was holding onto old clothes because she thought a full closet meant a luxurious wardrobe. She thought it made her feel prosperous. When she looked at all the leftovers, she realized the opposite was true and that her mother was right: quantity has nothing to do with quality. Not only was there no room for anything new, but because she had so many clothes Kate was not allowing herself to buy anything new. She didn't feel rich at all—she felt deprived. It seemed a contradiction: how could anyone with so much feel she had so little? Ironically, before going through her closets, most days Kate had a terrible time deciding what to wear because so many of her choices were unacceptable. It's hard to feel good about getting dressed when you're sure you're going to spend the rest of the day feeling awful about how you look. The fact of the matter is that we need only a few well-chosen outfits to feel we look smashing.

We were having lunch with Margaret. We asked her to try cleaning out her closet right there at the table. "Picture the clothes in your closet," we suggested. "Find one thing you never wear. Why do you still own it?"

"I can see myself standing in front of my packed closet, thinking I have nothing to wear. Oh, there's the first suit I bought after I got my MBA. I wore it to interviews while I was job hunting. I never wear it anymore because it doesn't fit me. Out of fashion, too. I guess I kept it as a souvenir. No, I think I've kept it because I thought it cost so much when I bought it that I had to wear it forever." She laughed. "Actually, I think I feel a little guilty every time I buy another suit. I can't quite convince myself that I ought to spend more money on suits. How silly!"

All of the items told some story about job interviews, trips planned and not taken, parties, funerals, memories both pleasant and unpleasant. "You know," she admitted, "it's no wonder I think I have nothing to wear. Every time I open my closet door, my past jumps out at me. Most of those clothes have nothing to do with the present."

What about you? What leftovers are you holding onto that make you feel like a leftover? Are you keeping things because they'll fit when you lose weight or gain some? If you haven't worn something for two years, and you're not on a diet, will it still be in style when you can fit into it again? Or does it seem to be scolding you every time you see it? Looking at clothes like that every morning is a real down: they make us feel terrible before we've had a chance to have breakfast!

Is your wardrobe consistent with your present life? Does it allow you to project the right message about who you are?

No matter how you do it, get rid of the clutter that causes confusion when you look in your closet.

Annette, an artist married to a prosperous attorney, told us, "I used to be very confused about what suited me. I would vacillate between dressing like a hippie and a lawyer's wife—whatever style that is. I sure didn't know but I thought I should. As a result, I felt schizophrenic: disloyal to whichever part of myself I was ignoring that day. Finally, when I couldn't stand it anymore, I began telling myself to pretend I was going out alone—just me—not as an artist, not as a lawyer's wife, just as a woman alone. Somehow that did the trick. Now I buy clothes because I like them, not because they fit some image. What a relief!"

Indeed, Annette has developed a distinctive style for herself. She looks terrific and she knows it.

* * *

Make sure the clothes you keep and the new ones you buy send out the right signals—the most important one being: "I'm a woman, and I like who I am."

Dressing for the Role of the Sexy Wife

Now, consider the clothes you own that are sexy, feminine, and glamorous. You may not want to wear them outside your home, but in order to play your role to the fullest you need some good costumes.

"When I decided that, in addition to my other roles in life, I wanted to be thought of as a sexy wife," Barbara recalls, "I was tentative about it. Whatever I did seemed so out of character that I felt silly. But I did it anyway. 'You don't have anything to lose,' I told myself. You know, nothing ventured, nothing gained. I wanted Rich to know I'd made a decision to be a sexy, glamorous wife. Of course, I was too embarrassed to just tell him, so I experimented with the best way to get my message across. I wondered what would happen if I told him I wanted a pink negligee with maribou feathers that I'd seen on the fourth floor of Saks. He said, 'So buy it.' 'That's not the sort of thing you buy for yourself,' I answered. I felt silly, but I waited. And he did indeed give it to me for my birthday. I was truly surprised. Until that moment, I hadn't been sure he was willing to play this new game with me. Now that I had the costume, I realized that I felt like an imposter. 'Me, sexy and glamorous?' I thought. 'I mean, I'm not Jennifer Beale or Rita Hayworth. I'm going to look ridiculous in this outfit.' I forced myself to put it on and sweep into the living room. I'm sure my face was as pink as the gown. I even told Rich how silly I felt. But I'm pleased to report that, silly or not, we had a great evening that was worth all the embarrassment."

Even though she felt awkward, Barbara's willingness to take a risk enabled her to change the tone of her relationship with Rich. She allowed herself to reveal an aspect of her personality that she had kept hidden. Rather than counting on subtle signs Rich might have read if the mood was right, she chose an overt theatrical gesture, one that really wasn't so out of character for her. Her husband has come to expect the unexpected from her, and now she knows he enjoys it.

You, too, can make a small change to send a big message that will let your husband know what you're up to. You don't need maribou for this, especially if you feel it's totally out of character. Instead, think about what you sleep in and what your bathrobe looks like. Do you like the way you look when you go to bed at night and make breakfast in the morning? If you don't think you're particularly attractive at those times, chances are your husband doesn't either.

Tonight sleep in something that will let both of you know how you feel. Choose one of his shirts or sexy underwear or nothing at all, and call his attention to what you're doing. Ask him if he minds if you borrow his shirt, and if he thinks the color you've chosen is flattering. Or tell him you found that sexy underwear buried in your bureau and decided it was a shame to waste it. Or tell him you don't need to wear clothes to bed because the heat of his body will keep you warm. In the morning wear his pajamas into the kitchen. Tell your kids you couldn't find your own bathrobe. (It doesn't matter what they think—they probably won't notice anyway.) Close your eyes and let your mind conjure a vision of how you'd like to look when you go to bed. Chances are good it will reveal the right gesture for you, one totally in character, yet totally new. Experiment with it. Find out what your husband thinks, see how long it takes him to notice. (If he doesn't notice after two weeks, have a serious talk with him about what is *not* going on between you.) Press through your embarrassment and find your own version of a negligee trimmed with maribou.

All of us care what other people think of us and how they judge us. Even men. Your husband may want to make some gesture, some change in his behavior or dress, and not know how or what. As you notice and evaluate your own coded signals, you will begin to notice your husband's. Although how he dresses does not reflect you, it is also true that when two people are in sync their physical appearance is harmonious as well. Some couples almost seem to share an aura or glide as if they were dancing. Even when they are only serving dinner to guests, they go together. Pay some attention to the styles your husband chooses. Have they changed since you've known him? Since he graduated from college? How long are his sideburns? Is he tenaciously clinging to leftovers or does his physical presentation reflect the man he has become? Robert Ponti, author of *Dressing to Win* and a leader of seminars on self-presentation, states that the length of a man's sideburns perfectly reflects how old he was when he thought he was really sexy. How long are your husband's sideburns? What image does he project? Is it appropriate?

You can help him to change his style of dressing at the same time you are making changes in your own. Begin gently. Don't attack; as you already know, that won't work. Instead, make small specific suggestions. When he is wearing clothes that you like and that flatter him, tell him exactly what you like and why. For example, let him know that his striped blue tie really complements his blue eyes. Or tell him that his new jeans fit so well you want to pat his behind. Don't tell him you hope he never wears his baggy jeans again because they're such a turn-off—tell him how good he looks in the new ones. Allow him to take another look at his underlying assumptions about his appearance just as you have done. The insidious power of unexamined assumptions and beliefs make them dangerous for all of us. When we take the time to examine the decisions reflected in our behavior, our dress, our whole way of being in the world, we become free to choose again. It may be that we'll choose to do nothing different and that's perfectly appropriate. It's the automatic action that is inappropriate and damaging. It limits possibilities and makes us prisoners of rules and regulations we didn't know were in force.

On Hearing Compliments

When was the last time you told your husband you thought he was one terrific guy? When was the last time you told him how much you like the way he looks or what a great person you think he is? Do you think he heard you or did he change the subject? All of us want to be complimented and acknowledged, yet when someone says exactly what we want to hear, most of us are so embarrassed we tune it out. Most people hear compliments through a fog of their own negative self-assessment—too old, too young, too wrinkled, too boring. Until we improve our self-esteem, it's hard to notice acknowledgments of any kind. We're simply too embarrassed. When you feel good about your physical presentation, compliments are easy to take.

Writing in *Psychology Today*, researchers Mark Knapp, Robert Hopper, and Robert Bell suggest that "how someone replies to a compliment is also related to self-esteem. We are more likely to accept compliments if they fit our own self-evaluation. Of course, we may like them even if we are suspicious of their accuracy or the motives behind them."

Remember, to have a love affair you must feel lovable, and you can't feel lovable if you can't hear what other people love about you. The people who love us want us to feel good about ourselves and feel frustrated if we don't respond to their praise. Your husband may think he's told you at least a million times how pretty, smart, sexy, and wonderful you are. Have you heard him? Or have you noticed only what he hasn't said? He says you're sexy, you want him to tell you you're a good cook. You want him to know you think he's handsome, he only wants to hear he's a good father. Where does that leave both of you? Having two different, highly dissatisfying conversations.

The next time your husband tells you he likes the way you look or that he loves your breasts (and you don't agree), don't change the subject, and don't tell him he is crazy or wrong. He is actually right because he's giving you his opinion, not asking for yours. When your husband pays you a compliment, listen to him instead of to the voice in your head that says, "What does he know?" Certainly, he knows what he likes better than you do. Knapp, Hopper, and Bell describe compliments as "a potentially threatening phenomenon that people seem to crave; a form of behavior that has powerful and positive effects on our personal and vocational lives; and an aspect of conversation that people experience every day yet still have trouble dealing with." Their research indicates that a compliment given is likely to be returned. Whether or not we agree, a compliment does make us feel good—so start practicing giving and receiving them.

Think of everything you like about your husband. Tell him. Tell him so he understands what you mean and that he hears you. Don't let him change the subject or walk away. It's likely that he'll respond by returning the compliment. If you tell him you love his body or some part of it, he'll find something about yours that he likes and tell you. That's the way compliments are given and received in our society. Notice how you feel when you're giving compliments; notice how you feel when you're receiving them. Flattery may not get you everything but it is, indeed, irresistible. The next time you glimpse your reflection in a mirror or a store window, remember to give yourself a compliment! Look at who you really are—a woman who has declared she will have a love affair with her husband.

"Great," you say. "Where is this flattering, passionate love affair going to take place? We have young children. My mother-in-law lives with us. We have no privacy. The bed is old and lumpy. Nobody has love affairs at home— too boring."

What can you do about it? If home is where the heart is, why not the passion?

Home Is Where
the Heart Is, So
Where's the Passion?

You have just redecorated your living room. Now it is the perfect room in which to have a love affair: spacious, elegant, yet warm and welcoming. There is a couch and a love seat covered in sensuous velvet. There is a deep lush carpet. The lighting is muted and throws off a pale peachy glow that is most flattering to your complexion—your skin looks soft and smooth and silky. Candlelight shimmers from mirrors and paintings. Music can be heard, but the equipment is hidden. There is space to dance and to sit close together and enough room in front of the fireplace to make love. Here you could have an afternoon tea for two, a romantic midnight supper, or an evening spent melting marshmallows and melting kisses. It's a room where you and your husband can spend time undisturbed, so you have added French doors that can be closed and locked.

For your first evening in this room you've arranged to be alone. You are wearing a gorgeous flowing silk kimono. A special dinner has been prepared, and the table set with your best linen, silver, and china. Candles are lit in the dining room and the living room. There is a fire in the fireplace, and a bottle of champagne cooling in an ice bucket next to the caviar on the coffee table. You hear his key in the front door and turn on the tape you've made especially for this evening. On it are all the songs that mean something to both of you. You lead him into the new room, pour the champagne and toast the new loving room you have created. You hold hands as you dine, make love in front of the fireplace for dessert, and end the evening wrapped in luxurious plush robes.

Have you ever thought of doing that in your living room? We bet you did once. We bet you used to spend a lot of time imagining how you would seduce him, how you would please him—and yourself. We bet that when you first fell in love, you turned every place you went into a love nest. It never occurred to you to create sexy scenes—they happened no matter where you were. Remember the couch in your parents' living room or the old swing on his parents' porch? Remember how dangerous the time you spent there seemed? At any moment a mother might appear and find the two of you locked together. Remember how illicit and exciting it all seemed? What mattered then was discovering each other's bodies, discovering how much you wanted each other, discovering the ecstasy you two could create for each other. No matter how often you were in each other's arms, you were never satisfied, it was never enough.

These days discovery and ecstasy don't seem to have anything to do with your lives. You've been paying a mortgage or rent on something you call home. Everything may be well matched and perfectly chosen; it may be the one place in the world where you are truly relaxed, and the best place to recover from the stresses and strains of the workaday world. But it doesn't remotely resemble a love nest. You can't imagine having a passionate affair there.

Romantic Settings and Taboos

To recapture that sense of impending discovery and ecstasy in order to have a love affair with your husband in your own home, you will have to challenge the unwritten and unspoken agreements you've made with him regarding sex and romance and the hours and places for it. You know, the rules that say you can't do "it" now because the kids are awake; or you're going to a business dinner and can't be late; or he has an early meeting and doesn't have time to fool around in the shower. You can't make love on the couch because it was so expensive, you can't make love on the porch swing because the neighbors might see, and you only make love in bed because anywhere else would seem adolescent. You've taken on your mother's role and made rules that restrict what you can and can not do. But it's your home now, and they're your rules. Isn't it time to break them and make new ones?

To get away from rules and your overly familiar, perhaps too expensive furniture, you could start over—move to another city or, better yet, another country. There, it would be a cinch to create a wonderful new, romantic, and sexy setting. You could pretend you'd just met and don't know who snores, who is irritable in the morning, and who, every now and then, falls into a twelve-hour coma in front of the TV. No one would know you, no one would have old ideas and judgments about you, and perhaps it would be easier to let go of your own. In this new place, you would find new friends who would only know you as that romantic new couple. They wouldn't be surprised if you put mirrors over the bed and slept on satin sheets and used the living room couch or the dining room table as often as the bed. Of course, they wouldn't know where or how often you made love, but you and your husband could make new rules and agreements without being inhibited by the perceptions you believe other people have of you.

For most people, moving is not an option; changing the rules is. To turn the spaces of ordinary life into the settings for love affairs, the old agreements and leftover decisions must be uncovered, then refurbished or rejected. Just as our dress mirrors how we view ourselves, so do our living spaces. And, like our clothing styles, our homes may not necessarily reflect who we are now. (Usually the two styles are somewhat consistent. Since you've just had practice making new decisions about your clothes, it will be easier to sort out those old decisions about your home that are preventing you from using it to its best, most sensuous advantage.) Long ago you made decisions that now define your behavior and what you are and are not allowed to do at home. When we set ourselves up to keep house we were focusing on our interpretation of "home." Now you want to focus on passion, and the old arrangements and agreements may simply not apply.

Are there rooms you always make love in? Never make love in? Can you imagine that you made an agreement about that? Are there agreements about which rooms you're allowed to have fun in and which are for the serious business of life? Can you picture the two of you locked in a passionate embrace in the dining room? Can you imagine yourself flirting your way through dinner? Can you imagine taking off your husband's tie as you clear the first course, then unbuttoning his shirt on your way to and from the kitchen? Why not? Remember, you're just imagining—you don't have to do it. But if thoughts like these never enter your mind, you have no chance at all of changing the rules, behaving differently, and finding another place where the two of you can play. Probably you are like the rest of us and don't realize that grown-ups need places to play just as children do. For that matter, is there any place in your home that is really yours in which you can do anything you choose?

We all make unspoken agreements with our mates: he takes out the garbage, you cook; you never eat dinner on the bed; you never watch TV while you're eating, you always watch TV when you're eating; he reads the newspaper at breakfast, you never have a serious conversation in the morning; you're responsible for making sure the kids keep their rooms clean, he's responsible for discipline; he walks the dog, you feed him; he makes travel arrangements, you do the packing; he takes care of his own clothes; he has a great sense of humor and you're his straight man; you never make love in the morning except on Sunday, and you only do it in the bedroom, on the bed. Start thinking about the agreements you have about your home. How much do they have to do with the way you want to live? When did you make them? What purpose did they serve and are they still relevant?

* * *

When Ellen and Sy got married, they didn't have much money. After long discussions, they decided to spend what they had on very good furniture for the living room because somewhere they'd heard that a well-built couch and chairs last a lifetime. The pieces were covered in a beautiful but sturdy fabric. "We were so thrilled with them," Ellen told us. "They made us feel grown-up and really married! But we were also afraid we'd do something to ruin them so we hardly went into the living room except on special occasions. Of course, we never made love on the couch—the thought never entered our minds. And, you know, we still have that couch, and we still don't use the living room except for special occasions. Isn't that ridiculous? We don't have to worry about money anymore, the kids aren't around much, and now I can't imagine why we're still living by those old rules."

The next time we saw Ellen, she told us that she'd seduced Sy in the living room. "It was so out of character and habit for us to be making love in that room! But it was refreshing and renewing. After all, it's our house, why shouldn't we do what we want in it?"

What about you? Are you using your home to its best advantage? Does it accurately reflect the people you and your husband have become?

Who Lives Here?

Look around your house as if you'd never seen it before. How would you describe the people who live there? What statement about them and their relationship does the furniture make? Are they young and poor? Young and successful? Middle-aged and successful? Middle-aged and disappointed with the way things turned out? Old, and so tired they've given up? Is the furniture traditional? Modern? Glitzy? Are the rooms neat and cozy or cozy and messy or just plain messy? Do they have a good time there or do the rooms seem unlived in? Can you detect signs that nothing sexy or playful ever happens there? Do you like what you see? What is unfinished or incomplete about this home? No matter how you answer, it's time to consider making the changes that will reflect the change in your attitude about yourself and your marriage—changes that will allow you to play and have a love affair whenever the mood strikes you.

We know. You've got lots of reasons why you can't, won't, or haven't changed so much as a vase or a picture or the position of a chair since you moved in:

1. I've moved the furniture around dozens of times, and the only place for it is exactly where it is.
2. We spent a lot of money on a decorator who was very good, and I'm not sure I could make any improvement.
3. Why bother? The kids are little and messy, the dog is old and messy, we're too busy to entertain, so it doesn't matter how the house looks.
4. We don't have enough money to refurbish or move or make any changes at all.
5. We bought very expensive furniture so it would last a lifetime—we can't change it, ever.

Relax. The changes we're going to suggest do not have to cost money. You won't have to take a course in interior design to make them nor will they disrupt your relaxed way of life—they will only enhance it. The truth is: If you maintain the status quo, you don't have room for anything else.

Your purpose is to revitalize your home and how you use it without spending a lot of money. Start small. Exchange the vases, ashtrays, and bowls on display with pieces you've kept in the cupboards. Put a bud vase in the bathroom where your husband shaves, candlesticks on the coffee table, an afghan on the sofa. Find the accessories that will evoke your first fling with your husband and display them prominently. Once the small touches are complete, look around the rooms to see if it's possible to rearrange the furniture to give your home a different flavor and ambience.

Harriet had been complaining for years about her living room. "It's not that I don't like the furniture or even its position. Well, maybe there is one large piece I'd like to replace, and a new piece is not in our budget. It's just that the room has looked the same for ten years. I'm so bored with it that I'll come up with any excuse to avoid being in there. We hardly entertain anymore. And make love in there? You've got to be kidding."

"You don't have a very large apartment," we reminded her. "It's a shame that you don't use the whole space."

"Well, let me take another look. Maybe I'll see a possibility I've missed."

Harriet called to tell us she'd found one piece of furniture she could move out of the living room that enabled her to rearrange everything else. "I kept shoving things around till I'd created two distinct spaces in the room. Then I put away all the modern objects that had been on display and replaced them with my grandmother's crystal bowls, vases, and ashtrays. I feel like I've moved to a country house. I know that sounds silly, the changes are really so small, but that's how I feel. And Roger and I have been listening to Mozart and smooching in there after the kids are asleep. It's given us both a lift. We also started looking for an armoire to replace our old bookshelves. And it's been fun rummaging in antique stores together."

You may be like Harriet and need to take another look. What small change would make a big difference? Do it.

Living Room Or Loving Rooms

No matter how difficult you think it will be, no matter how frightening the thought, plan to make love in the living room, then the den or the family room, then the dining room, then the kitchen—in other words, in absolutely every room in your home. There are three very good reasons for including these rooms as settings for your love affair:

1. This is your home—you have a right to use it in any way you choose.
2. You'll never forget that you did.
3. Making love in rooms other than your bedroom will allow you to feel that sense of danger and daring you once felt when you did something illicit before you were married.

If you have a large family living under one roof or only one child, you will have to plan ahead to accomplish this. You could set your alarm clock for three in the morning, but it might be easier to wait until the kids go to school or to camp. If you think you should wait until they're in college, and they're only seven and nine, think again!

Begin in the room that most clearly reminds you of when you were just getting to know your husband. Choose your moment, just as you did in the old days. Perhaps it will be after a dinner party or after Monday night football when the kids are sure to be asleep. If the TV is in the living room, it will be very easy to bring your husband some tea, a brandy, or a beer just as the game is ending. Sit very close to him on the couch or crawl into his lap (remember the purring pussycat?). Make sure you are fully dressed, just as you were when you were first dating. Remember, the point here is to re-create some of the excitement and intrigue you once felt, so if you feel embarrassed don't worry about it. That's how you felt then. Now, pretend you've never done this before with this man in this space—and if you've never necked in your own living room, den, or family room, you won't have to pretend. Notice where you want to touch him and where you want to be touched. Guide his hands. Talk to him. Tell him how good it feels to be close to him.

Willy and Lee told us about the first night they made love on the couch. "We're not sure how it started," Lee said. "Our kids were still quite young. In fact, we were sharing the master bedroom with the baby. I guess it seemed more private on the couch. So there we were, without a stitch on, having a wonderful time when Lizzie called, 'Mommy!' The possibility of being discovered was nerve-racking and titil-lating but being able to make love that way reminded us how much we excite each other. Do you know, after Lizzie went back to sleep, we went back to the couch. We haven't forgotten that night and how it heightened our love mak-ing, so we re-create it often."

Or set the stage for a dance party—just for the two of you. Find the records or tapes that were part of your court-ship. Put them on after dinner, after the kids are asleep, after the dishes, the newspaper, the late news. You don't have to dance all night—just for one song, just long enough to get him into your arms. And, as you move to the music, start taking off his clothes. Take off your own. In time to the music, lead him to a place where you can be romantic and sexy. Remember, it's okay to feel embarrassed—it's worth the risks.

Once you have become adept at seducing your husband in the living room, den, or family room, he'll catch on to the sexy games you're playing and will make up some of his own.

Creating the Unexpected

Remember when you were first married, how every time you started cooking, your husband would sidle up to you, put his arms around you while you were peeling carrots, and nuzzle your neck? Remember how annoyed you used to get. "Not now," you'd chide. "Your parents are coming for dinner! I want to impress them." Or it was your first dinner party, and you were nervous about the chocolate mousse. Or your friends from work were coming for brunch, and you'd never made eggs benedict before. Whatever the reason, you made it clear to your husband that the kitchen was off limits for snuggling, and he should stay out unless he was going to help. And, since he didn't like being rebuffed, he obeyed you. He may even have become a superb chef, but he has left snuggling off the menu. Now, remember when you were just dating. If that sexy guy followed you into the kitchen and put his arms around you, we bet you thought it was great and turned you on instead of you turning him away.

It's time to take a new look at your old kitchen. Time to make a new agreement about what's appropriate "kitchen behavior." Think of a reason to call your husband into the kitchen. (You can always use the old standby: "Honey, could you open this jar?") While he's working on it, wrap your arms around him and tell him he looks handsome or feels so strong. He'll be surprised but he'll love it. Or ask him to get something from the top shelf that you can't reach. When he's up on the step ladder, stroke his thigh or rub his backside. Women who are having affairs entice like this all the time. Why not you? When he gets off the ladder, make sure you're right there to give him a warm sexy hug. You know the kind we mean: pelvis against pelvis. Next time, ask him to help you down from the ladder—especially if you're wearing something that shows off your legs. By this time he'll realize the only rule in the kitchen is: anything goes.

If you think about it, you'll realize that the kitchen is the perfect semipublic place to carry on a seduction: no one expects you to make advances to your husband there, so no one will notice except him. If you have guests in the living room they'll never suspect, and if the kids are helping you they won't notice. If they do, think of yourselves as providing a positive role model for marriage: people who love each other express affection openly. Once you have regained the kitchen as a romantic setting, mundane chores can become preludes instead of battle cries.

Baths and Showers

Plan an evening in the bathtub with your husband. Invite him formally or at the last minute, whichever will guarantee his company. The first rule is don't fill the tub as you would if you were bathing alone—two bodies take up more space than one. Second, use bubble bath that really foams or drops of scented oil, your favorite perfume or his aftershave will do. Third, make sure to have lots of fluffy towels within easy reach. Consider bringing some candles into the bathroom along with wine, champagne, brandy, or his favorite drink—and an erotic book (see the bibliography for some suggestions).

Once you're in the tub together (you may have to maneuver for a comfortable position but don't give up, eventually you'll find it) sink into the water and relax. Your purpose is to create sensual pleasure and sexual tension, not to have intercourse. Notice how good the water feels against your skin, how his body feels underwater. Notice how smooth and silky you both feel. Imagine yourself being petted and stroked by the most sensuous lover in the world. You may even want to run your hands slowly over your own body and his. Do it. You may feel so relaxed that you'll want to tell him what you're thinking about. Tell him. Give yourself permission to be turned on and to turn him on.

When you get out of the tub, give him a rubdown and ask him to do the same for you. You will need baby oil or some other more exotic massage oil. Turn the lights down low in your bedroom or light the room with scented candles. Play your favorite music. Invite your husband to lie down on the bed. Start your massage as far from his most erotic spots as possible. If his feet are ticklish, don't touch them. As you move your hands over his body, tell him what you are doing, describe how he looks to you. As you get closer and closer to his erogenous zones, increase the pressure of your fingers and keep talking about what you are touching. Don't neglect his buttocks or his nipples or the side of his neck. Use all your knowledge of his body till he is as ready as you've ever seen him. Now tell him it's your turn. Then go to bed and to sleep. In Chapter 5, we discussed how massage can be part of the process of appreciating your body and his. Here your purpose is to turn him on, to be turned on, to torture each other into ecstasy. The Japanese have developed massage techniques that enhance sexual pleasure into a game in which the loser is the one who climaxes first (see *Shibumi* by Trevanian). Which one of you will be the winner in your game? And whatever happens, be a good loser.

If you haven't joined your husband in the shower in years, start again. Surprise him in the morning or evening. As soon as you get in, take the soap and wash his body. Do it slowly and thoroughly so there'll be lots of lather. And, as you wash each part, talk to him about his legs, his buttocks, his penis, his back, his chest, his arms, his neck, and his face. If he takes a morning shower, you'll send him off to work in a very cheerful mood—it won't hurt yours either. If he takes a shower before bed, follow the same routine recommended for long, lingering baths.

Your Bedroom—Everybody's Haven

Your bedroom should be a very special room. It should be a place where you and your husband go to escape everything and everyone else. It should be private; it should be perfection. But how many bedrooms are like that? Possibly your fourteen-year-old daughter's is, but what about yours? Just for fun, we made a list of all the activities that generally take place in the master bedroom:

1. Eat breakfast, lunch, or dinner.
2. Hold family conferences.

3. Watch football, baseball, hockey, basketball, tennis, golf, the Olympics, the Academy Awards, presidential speeches, and other special events. The watchers may include your entire family, their friends, and assorted relatives.
4. Help the children do homework.
5. Do your own work.
6. Write letters and pay bills.
7. Get dressed and undressed.
8. Put sick children to bed.
9. Be sick in bed yourselves.
10. Read.
11. Sleep.
12. Make love.

You may not do all these things in your bedroom, but chances are you do most of them. Indeed, you probably have a busier bedroom than we do. Even if the rest of your home becomes a romantic setting for your affair, it's important to ensure that your bedroom is *your* haven—and yours alone. Your first step is to put a lock on your door if you don't have one. Your second step is to make some new rules with your children about privacy. Unless they are under five they've probably invented their own rules for keeping you out of their rooms; certainly you deserve the same luxury. You can put vaseline on the outer doorknob, as one couple did, or use a "Do not disturb" sign from your last stay in a hotel or make your own sign that says, "Knock before entering." Or, if you don't feel up to calligraphy, ask one of your kids to make the sign for you. However you do it, make it clear to them that you respect their privacy and that they must respect yours. If they won't, you won't. To most children, this will seem a fair trade.

Now that your privacy is assured, is your bedroom a room in which you want to be alone with your husband? Is there a corner with two comfortable chairs where you can sit together and talk or have a drink or coffee? Is it time to rearrange the furniture or buy new sheets or a new spread or some fluffy new pillows? Have you thought about putting a pair of candlesticks in the bedroom or buying a scented candle that matches your favorite perfume? These are small touches that evoke romance.

Would you be willing to put a mirror on the ceiling? No? Not surprising, neither would most of us. But how about adding more mirrors around the room? You probably already have a full-length mirror and one over your bureau. But does he have one over his bureau or is there one near the bed for nighttime routines? Mirrors can be added easily, and they create a special effect. Candles shimmer in them romantically. They offer tantalizing glimpses of your most tantalizing parts. Best of all, your friends and relatives won't give them a second thought. Their real use can be your secret.

Before you turn off the lamps, light the candles. Start making love before you reach the bed and move toward the full-length mirror instead. Wrap yourself around him from behind so that you can see both your faces. As you hold and stroke each other, watch yourselves in the mirror. Watch your faces and your hands. Look in his eyes; look in your own. Watch how your faces change; your eyes soften and glisten. Be a voyeur, watching lovers you know well. If you feel you can't be so bold the first time, tilt the mirror across the room so that you can see yourselves from the bed. Watch your reflections and call his attention to them.

Bedded Bliss

The marriage bed is a symbol of marital fidelity, togetherness, solace, and comfort. It can be a secret weapon for
good mischief or for prolonging a fight or starting one.
When you're having an argument, you can each sleep on
opposite edges and never touch or you can join him on his
side if you want to tell him that your part of the fight is over.
When filmmakers want to suggest passion they pan the
camera across a double bed, and when children are fright-
ened or sick, they climb in; ditto the dog or the cat. They
know a good thing when they see it. In our collective cultu-
ral memory we associate double beds with wedding nights,
childbirth, and death. And, for most of us, our first double
bed meant we were grown up.

Winnie remembers the first king-size bed she slept in.
"It was my wedding night and I thought if I climbed in,
I'd be lost. When the bedspread was removed I was re-
lieved to see that it was just two twin beds pushed together. John and I only used one; we messed up the other
so the maid would think we'd used both. Now, of course,
the idea of such a large bed seems like heaven. When all
three kids and the dog climb in, it seems like there's not
enough room."

On the other hand, when Julie and Dave needed to
replace their fifteen-year-old mattress they gave some
thought to getting a larger bed. "But, in the end," Julie told
us, "I decided I liked the standard double size the best.
What do we need more room for—to get further apart
when we're not speaking? I like being crowded and cozy,
and a small bed sort of forces us to make up faster."

*   *   *

Whatever size bed you prefer, make sure it's the size you're sleeping in. If it's not, spend the money right now to buy the one you want. Saving money on this important piece of furniture will not save (or strengthen) your marriage. If you spend money on nothing else, spend it on your bed. Buy silk or satin sheets, if you want them, or a luxurious comforter and lacy pillows or a mohair throw. Indulge yourself. Buy something for your bed that reemphasizes its importance in your lives. Then plan to use that bed in a new way. Challenge your husband to a weekend—or at least part of one—in bed. Buy your favorite foods and some good books; rent a sexy movie for your VCR or buy a book of erotic photographs; practice giving each other massages; sleep a lot and make love a lot. You may decide you like doing that more than going to Paris for the weekend. And think of the money you'll save!

Rules and Regulations

Human beings are creatures of habit. Everybody knows that husbands and wives don't spend the weekend in bed together unless they're sick. Everybody knows that men sleep closest to the door. Everybody assumes that the hostess sits in the chair nearest the kitchen. Everybody has their own place in each room. They gravitate to those same places over and over again. Don't you always sit in the same chair in your living room? Does everybody have a specific place at the dinner table? Or a chair or a spot on the floor for watching TV? What would happen if you made some changes?

At dinner tonight put place cards on the table and mix up your family. Sit next to your husband instead of across from him. Call attention to the new places—get everyone to notice the habits they've formed. Let them know that if you sit in the same place all the time, your point of view is likely to be limited, and you've decided that seeing things from another angle is interesting and exciting. Let one of your children sit in your place and your husband's. Sit in your husband's place and watch TV. Be in his chair in the living room when he comes home from work. Take out the garbage if that's his job. Walk the dog if he usually does. Ask him to pack for you, instead of packing for him. Make the travel arrangements for your next trip and surprise him. Make sure you've uncovered all the unspoken agreements you've made with your husband that inhibit having a love affair with him in your own home.

What you want is results! Not explanations or reasons or evidence. It doesn't matter why something works, as long as it works. What results are you having in your love affair with your husband?

How Often Do You Make Love These Days and Who's Counting?

You and your husband have a standing lunch date on Mondays. You go to the movies, just the two of you, and neck. On Tuesdays you meet for drinks and a massage in a hotel or motel room nearby. You never go back to the same one until you have run out of choices. On Wednesdays you read erotic poetry or stories to each other when you go to bed. You don't make love on Wednesday—ever —you just read about what other people do. When you wake up on Thursday mornings, you take a long bath together. Neither of you ever makes early-morning appointments for Thursday so you won't have to rush out of the house. And you are so turned on by what you read the night before that you simply can't wait to get into the tub together. On Fridays you invite your single friends for dinner. There are always two people in the group you think will get along very well together. Watching their sparks fly turns you on. You spend Saturdays planning a surprise for each other—you might choose a racy movie for the VCR, dress for dinner in the outfit you were wearing when you met, or he might cook only your favorite foods (the ones that mean love to you). And on Sundays you spend as much of the day in bed—alone together—as possible, but no less than three hours. You don't have to count how often you make love because, one way or another, you make love every day. You know that making love is more than how often you actually have intercourse. You both look ten years younger than you really are, and everyone wants to know your secret. Some people have been unable to control themselves—they ask bluntly how many times a week you have sex. You know they're trying to compete with you, and you're not giving away any of your secrets.

Before you got married, you were warned (like the rest of us) about what would eventually happen to your sex life. You were told that if you put a bean in a jar every time you made love during your first year of marriage and removed one every time you made love thereafter, you'd never empty the jar. "What a gruesome idea!" you thought. "That is never going to happen to us! I'll do anything to avoid it."

And you were right. Sex in marriage is not a contest, and it definitely has nothing to do with counting beans! Your statistics won't be entered in the *Guinness Book of World Records*. Nobody but you really cares how often you make love these days. Besides, counting beans may obscure what's really going on.

* * *

Samantha discovered the hard way that she was counting the wrong beans. "I had been single for a long time," she told us. "When I got married for the second time, I found myself keeping track of how many times a week Bob and I made love, just like I did before I felt secure about our relationship. When it seemed infrequent, I drove myself crazy wondering if he thought I was too old, too wrinkled, and if he'd found a younger woman and was having an affair. Then I began to nag Bob. I created an enormous amount of pressure and tension, and an entire month went by during which neither of us touched the other. Unfortunately, I had to hit bottom before I could convince myself that if he was going to leave me, he would, and I'd survive. I also realized that before we got married I had used how often he wanted to make love as a measure of how much he cared for me, and I was still doing that. As soon as I relaxed, so did he. We make love quite often now. It's clear to me that if we don't feel any pressure about sex, we're free to do it or not. And since we are very attracted to each other, it just happens. I guess you have to be willing to let it be okay no matter what."

Samantha realized that her interpretation of their sexual frequency statistics was inaccurate, created unnecessary tension, and had nothing to do with love making. Nevertheless, she's not alone in this. Sex sometimes feels more like an Olympic competition than an act of love. From the first moment we discover sex we become combatants—boys against girls, girls against girls, boys against boys. When we get older we don't discuss the details (well, certainly not very many and not very often), but we continue to keep a sharp eye out for which women seem sexier, which couple seems to be "doing it" more than we are, and who might be the best lover. Even if we have sex lives that fulfill our fantasies, we remain curious about everybody else. How often are they "doing it"? Do they know something we don't? Are we missing something? Most of us, whether or not we admit it, want to know what the norm is, and then we want to know how to "do it" more, better, and differently.

Are You Normal and How Do You Know?

Being informed about the range of normal sexual behavior is reassuring and helps to allay our anxieties. Dr. Sy Silverberg, Director of the Canadian Institute for Sex Research in Toronto, told us "Everyone wants to know what constitutes normal sexual activity. It's one of the first questions my clients ask me." To determine if there is a norm for sexual behavior, Dr. Silverberg developed a questionnaire that he mailed to sex therapists (because they are supposed to know more than the rest of us) throughout the U.S. and Canada. His study, as yet unpublished, confirms that everything is normal—or nothing is: sex therapists behave just as we do. Their responses indicate that there is no "normal" behavior; there is only what turns us on and is satisfying.

Doing research is like counting beans: scientists agree that research has to be quantifiable in order to be useful, therefore research regarding sexual behavior is expressed in numerical terms. Carol Botwin in *Is There Sex After Marriage?*, cites studies indicating that the "honeymoon" phase of sexual activity lasts about two years and that thereafter frequency falls by roughly fifty percent. In one study, forty-five percent of the men and women questioned had sex three times a week during their first two years of marriage; only twenty-five percent had sex three times a week in the second through eighth years of marriage. Most married people experience similar stages over the years and have difficulty adjusting to the posthoneymoon diminution of passion.

Sex *is* different when you're married. That's a fact. The chase is over. You have each other. The tension of not knowing how it will end can't be re-created. You don't have to worry if he'll call; you don't have to worry if you're too pushy. You don't have to make love each time as if it might be the last. You know it won't be. Still, we use the same standards to judge the quality of sex. And it is an erroneous comparison. As Alexandra Penney points out in *Great Sex*, "For most people, frequency refers to the number of times the penis goes into the vagina." This standard of frequency excludes all the other forms of sexual pleasure: touching, cuddling, licking, massaging, hugging, talking, and being close and comfortable, warm and loving with another human being. Sadly, when we count how many times we've "done it," we rarely include these activities that are so essential to an ongoing sensual and enduring relationship.

While statistics may provide some comfort—now we know we're normal—they also set a standard by which we can (and do) measure ourselves. And the numbers seem to prove that marriage inevitably means reduced sexual satisfaction—that a sensual, sexy love affair with your husband is highly unlikely. We have learned to have negative expectations of sex in marriage, and these color our vision of what it is like to live with the same person for many years. In the process, the jar of beans is never emptied. Instead, we collect more evidence to support the thesis that marriage equals less frequent, less enjoyable, possibly stale sex. We fail to notice any evidence that disproves this theory. Statistics of any kind can only measure past behavior—what was, not what can be. Statistical data do not measure what is possible nor do they measure the quality of love making; they only measure the quantity.

Although scientific evidence confirms that after the first two years of marriage the frequency of intercourse declines for seventy-five percent of couples, what about the other twenty-five percent? What has enabled them to ignore or defy the statistics? Have they noticed that they are far more competent lovers now than when they first began? Do they take advantage of their skills? Are they less serious about it? Have you ever noticed how intense people become when they talk about their so-called sexual problems?

What Are Your Expectations?

Whose idea was it to count beans in the first place? Who told the first joke about wives who get headaches to avoid sex? Why aren't there any jokes about husbands? What if everyone agreed that sex is dull and boring until you get married? What if headache jokes were only told about mistresses and paramours—never wives? What if we were warned that instead of never emptying the jar after the first year of marriage, we'd need a bigger jar every year? Our expectations about marital sex would certainly be very different from what they are now.

What were your sexual expectations when you got married? Did your vision become a reality? How is it different? Did you have some idea of how a romantic husband would behave? Does your husband behave the way you want him to? Or is he romantic in his own way, and therefore you don't notice? If your husband calls you several times during the day to ask questions or tell you silly jokes, are you annoyed? Or do you realize that he is flirting with you? Think about it. If silly jokes are not part of your vision of romance, you may be missing something. Many men do not get the acknowledgment they deserve because the women in their lives have different notions of what constitutes "being romantic." The women simply do not notice what is really going on because it doesn't fit their ideas.

"Ridiculous," you're thinking. "Nobody is that dense."

It's actually worse than that. There are some people who don't even notice when they are sexually aroused. An article in *The New York Times* reported on a study measuring physiological changes as related to sexual guilt. Levels of sexual arousal can be measured by monitoring changes in heartbeat, dilation of the pupils, color and temperature of the genitals. Women who expressed the most guilt at viewing erotic material were identified as having the most extreme physiological changes. These women were actually unaware that they were sexually aroused—they had successfully blocked their physical sensations as they were being recorded by researchers. The women were turned on, and they didn't know it! Apparently, the potential for sexual pleasure must be presented in ways that fit our images of how and when we think we should be aroused sexually or we miss it entirely. If we don't notice what is happening in our own bodies, we run the risk of diminishing our sensual experiences. What sensations and opportunities are you missing?

(If, indeed, you do have a long-standing sexual problem, if you think you're frigid or he is impotent, if intercourse hurts, if he suffers from premature ejaculation or priapism—continuous erection, usually caused by a disease—see your internist and/or a sex therapist. At once. There is a good chance that you can solve the problem since, according to Dr. Silverberg, most sexual dysfunctions are not physiological. Contact the American Association of Sex Educators, Counselors, and Therapists for names of professionals in your area.)

Reinventing Your Sex Lives

He complains that you are never in the mood or you don't move or you lie there like a dead fish. He refers endlessly to how often you used to make love and how infrequently you do now. You can't bear it that he makes love exactly the same way each time—he is drawn like a magnet to the spots he discovered oh, so long ago. He's the most unromantic person in the world and the most unwilling to discuss his feelings. You want tender romance; he wants frequency. You want orgiastic love making; he wants you to jog on your back. But enough of what was; it's time to create new possibilities.

Begin by noticing how it feels when you are getting turned on and where you feel it. Don't assume you know anything about your reactions so that you can really observe yourself. Notice how you know that you're in the mood. Pay attention to every little feeling, thought, or emotion you have regarding sex. What do you think turns you on? Is it, in fact, what turns you on? How do you know? Where does the feeling start? Does it begin in your belly, your arms, your legs, or in your head? What was the sexiest thought you ever had? Are you ready to tell him? As you become more aware of your own sensuality, share it with your husband.

Create new possibilities by talking to him about making love—but only in places where it is impossible to do anything about it.

"Jack and I have the best sex on airplanes," Terry confided, "because we use the time to have conversations about preposterous things we're going to do to each other as soon as we can. While we keep our voices low, we both imagine that someone is eavesdropping—listening to every one of our wild fantasies. We tell each other exactly where and how we'd like to touch each other. Then we imagine what would happen if we did any of it right there in our seats. We turn each other on so much that we can hardly stand it."

"Do you ever do anything on the plane besides talk?" we asked her.

"No, never. But we work ourselves up to a fever pitch, and we can't wait to be alone. We love the game—it's our secret. Of course, talking about sex really is a turn-on."

Indeed, there is nothing more erotic than being turned on and having to postpone pleasure, so instead of counting how often you make love, find times to tease each other. Follow up but don't follow through. Make up new rules: no hands; only one of you can move; no intercourse; keep all your clothes on. This is not a contest, so stop keeping score. Instead, relax and enjoy the freedom you have to explore new sensual experience.

"Steven and I were really having a tough time a few years back," Carol admitted. "Then I remembered an affair I had before I met my husband. I was really attracted to this man, but his kids were sleeping in the next room, which was very awkward for me. Oh yes, we kissed and touched each other, but no intercourse. I simply refused. Well, we were both so turned on all night (and all the next day) that we could hardly stand the tension until we could be alone. Those few days were a sexual high point for me. 'How can I create that for me and Steven?' I wondered. It seemed a little artificial since we were married and sleeping in the same bed. 'On the other hand,' I thought, 'why not give it a try?' The next night as Steven undressed, so did I. Then I made him sit in the chair in our bedroom so I could sit on his lap. I told him that we couldn't "do it" tonight, we could only practice. At first he thought I was joking, but it was an irresistible game. What a night! We did everything we could think of but . . . Since then, we don't need any excuses to play that game. We just do it from time to time. And not knowing which one of us is going to set the rules keeps us both on our toes. I recommend it."

Call it practice, not the real thing. Become experts at your own sensuality. Pay attention to all the signals your bodies send. Especially be aware of the ideas you have about sex; they influence your physical reactions more than anything else.

Sleeping Together

Do you sleep better with him or without him? Tell the truth. Aren't you used to having that warm cuddly body there, right next to you, in the middle of the night? Haven't you noticed that you miss him when either of you is away? Have you noticed how well you fit each other whether you curl around him or he curls around you? Aren't you used to falling asleep that way? We aren't talking about romance or sex now, just good old-fashioned being close to someone you love, someone you can hug. When was the last time you told him how you feel? If it was last night, good for you. If it wasn't, tell him tonight. If you aren't specific, he won't know how much you appreciate him. Give yourselves the gift of really noticing how wonderful it is to be in bed together.

Fine-tune your expanding skills of observation and awareness. Cuddle, curl, sniff, rub, touch, taste, and look. Notice it all. You never have to sleep in a cold empty bed. You always have a warm and potentially responsive body right there. Notice what your positions are when you wake up. You've paid a lot of attention to how things don't work between you. Why not play fair and give attention to what really does work? How close together do you sleep? Could you move closer? What would happen if you did? What would happen if you moved your hands over his body exactly as he moves his on yours? Try touching him in the same places and in the same way he touches you. Move your body exactly as he does. Do to him exactly what he's doing to you, at the same speed, at the same rhythm. You won't have to tell him what you're doing; you won't have to say a word. Try it tonight and see what happens.

Can you spend an extra few minutes in bed together in the morning and create a sense of renewal for yourselves? A few minutes alone, together, before the day begins is peaceful and energizing. Try it.

At night, change sides—move over to his. Start in a subtle way. The space will be warm and smell like him. When he takes your place, it will smell like you. The next step is to tell him you want to sleep on his side of the bed. You have an opportunity to revolutionize your whole nighttime routine. And if you can't sleep because you're not in the "right" place, don't. Make love. That's what Tina and Les do.

"I'm not sure how it really began," Tina related. "I do know that during our honeymoon, every time I woke up I was on a different side of the bed. Neither of us ever staked out a place. Then we discovered that most people do pick one side or the other, like a permanent parking spot. To celebrate our flexibility, we bought two alarm clocks and two phones so neither of us would be inconvenienced, and we're not stuck in a routine. I have to admit that we feel a little superior to everyone else. They don't know what they're missing!"

What are you ready to do tonight that you've never done or said to your husband before? You're two-thirds of the way into this book, and unless you've covered it with plain brown paper, your husband must have noticed what you're reading. For sure, you've begun to think of some new ways of being with him that hadn't occurred to you before. At dinner you could slip him an invitation to a late date or, if he is usually the one to suggest that you make love, take the first steps yourself. But whatever you do, take the time to notice your body and how it feels, notice the thoughts you have about your love making. If you are experiencing any sort of sexual malaise, just noticing that's how you feel is the first step out of it. Notice every time one of you makes an old familiar gesture or repeats a worn-out phrase. How many gestures and phrases are old and familiar? Can you stop yourself from repeating them? See if you can find a new move or another word. Find out which routines you don't want to give up because they give you so much pleasure; then stop referring to those actions as old and worn-out because they're not—they work. Then, make up new ones.

Notice every time you kiss each other and how many different ways you kiss. Find a new way to kiss each other. Every time you touch, be aware of your sensations. Be aware of how he tastes and smells. Notice how he looks during the day and how often your response to his looks changes. Notice that sometimes you think he looks handsome, sometimes tired, sometimes like a little boy, sometimes old or forbidding, sometimes warm and open. Notice how his voice sounds and how you think you can tell his moods from his tone. Notice the times when the sound of his voice is exciting to you and when it makes you feel loved. Be aware of how often during the day you think of him and how many times a day you do or say something that affirms your love for him. And, if you notice that he occasionally irritates you, don't worry. You can feel irritated and still notice that you are in the midst of a love affair with your husband.

Now, start counting how often you make love these days. Count every time you find another way to kiss, touch, hold, caress, fondle, or simply be together. Count every time you think of something good about him and every time you tell him. Count every time you get a sexy urge, feel a sexy swell somewhere in your body. They're your statistics; count everything.

9

Fantasy, the Fuel of Love

Against her bare skin the silk lining of her coat felt unfamiliar and yet comforting. In some indefinable way, she realized, it had the touch of a lover almost. The movement of her walking caused the silk to caress softly her naked breasts and to brush lightly against her thighs and the cheeks of her bottom. She thought that she would feel cold, but she did not. The truth was the unaccustomed touch of the coatlining on her body and the incredible fact of walking about in a state of concealed nakedness—and with a man who knew—these conspired to arouse her eroticism and to make her flushed and warm. . . . Her state of mind was no secret— Pierre understood well enough. . . . Her open mouth and staring eyes told him all that he needed to know—she was almost in a state of ecstasy from the touch of her coat on her bare body and the wild imaginings brought on by her nakedness. . . . (*Joie d'Amour: An Erotic Memoir of Paris in the 1920's* by Anne-Marie Villefranche)

Can you imagine yourself doing something as outrageous as putting on a satin-lined coat with nothing underneath and taking a walk with your husband? Are you among the small number of people who have no difficulty creating a wild, sexy fantasy and then acting it out? If so, you are lucky. Some of us are so embarrassed by sexual fantasies that we don't allow ourselves to have them at all; some are embarrassed to admit that we do have them while others are at least willing to admit it, but are too embarrassed to act them out. Perhaps we'd be less so if we noticed that the ways we entertain ourselves—how we plan dinner parties, our anticipation of birthdays, anniversaries, holidays, how we dress for formal occasions and costume parties—are clues to how adept at and comfortable we are with creating fantasies. We don't usually call that kind of social planning creating a fantasy. Nevertheless, every time we create a vision of an event, it is a fantasy until the event takes place. Having a sexual fantasy and acting it out is only an extension of the social planning most of us do every day of our lives. And while the planning of the event may create some anxiety, stepping out of our accustomed roles can be very pleasurable.

Robert Solomon reminds us that fantasy is one of the most crucial components of romantic love. "Fantasy, not music," Solomon says, "is the fuel of love." He points out that we do not love a person because of what we know about them but because of what we select and then idealize. In other words, we create a fantasy about the loved one. The moment we begin to experience being in love we use all the rich resources of our minds and imaginations. We explore what would have allowed us to meet sooner than we did, we imagine being together in exotic places as well as the ordinary ones that seem so special when we are first in love. We describe our lovers in ways that may seem farfetched and certainly strain the limits of credibility. We fantasize the ways we will experience our love: we dream of idyllic, musky, sex-slick nights of endless rapture. If there are difficulties to overcome, our imaginations work overtime to smooth the way. And when we get married, we forget about the richness of our imaginations and our ability to create fantasies. The fantasy that Solomon refers to is the one that allowed you to choose each other. The fantasy that we are referring to is the one that will enable you to enjoy the people each of you has become during the years you've been together and to get in touch with your own rich imaginations. Without reinvoking our ability to imagine new ways to express love, the mundaneness of married life would defeat us.

So, get ready to be incredible. If you are not willing to leave your home wearing nothing but a luxuriously lined coat, don't. Wear it at home instead. Before you go to bed, put the coat on and wander around in the privacy of your bedroom.

Notice how the lining feels against your skin; notice the weight of the coat on your body. Notice how sensual you feel. See if you can become aroused by the mere thought of it. Then, venture further into this fantasy. Find your husband and tell him what you are doing. Does the thought turn him on? Sit on his lap and ask him. Don't let him look. Keep the coat close around you. Don't let him check to see if you're really nude. Let him just think about it. And talk to him, whisper in his ear. Play with him.

Jenny tried it. "It was the evening I got my first fur coat. We were planning to drive a friend home after dinner so before we left the house, I took off all my clothes except my pantyhose. Then I put on the coat. I told Robert as we were walking out. I could tell that his first reaction was disbelief. The three of us continued to chat until we dropped off our friend. As soon as we were alone, we stopped talking. Instead, we stole quick glances at each other. I had an entirely new sense of my own body encased in the cool silk lining. By this time, I could tell that Robert was intrigued and turned on by the thought of my being almost naked. It was thrilling. I haven't done it again; I'm not sure it's an act you can repeat. But Robert and I talk about it, and the memory has the same effect each time."

Marriage counselors often recommend fantasy as a way to heighten pleasure in a long-term relationship. The most recent research indicates that people are more likely to be attracted to each other in a setting of mystery and tension. Clearly, acting out a fantasy is an easy way to create intrigue. The fantasies do not have to be extreme or farfetched. You don't have to imagine yourselves having intercourse in a public place or engaged in some outrageous encounter. Indeed, for many people fantasies like that aren't stimulating at all. The fantasies we're talking about are easy to act out because they are simple, basic, and can be part of your daily routines.

Nina and Leonard frequently pretend they've just met and talk to each other as if they are new lovers discovering each other. "I can't remember how it started," Nina said, "but one day I realized that we were playing together in a new way. Telling each other silly things and asking a lot of questions as if we didn't know everything there was to know about each other. Actually, we keep discovering new things—ideas, thoughts, experiences that somehow we haven't yet shared. We go into this routine at cocktail parties. It's become a great escape for us, and it sets us up for later, when we are alone.''

Lisa and Will have created Special Wednesdays. "We've set aside one day every week to do something unusual together. One of us plans it and doesn't tell the other. We picked Wednesdays because it's the low point of the week. Once, Will packed a bag for me and arranged a sitter for the kids. I've checked us into a local motel, sent flowers and telegrams, and we've had special dinners.''

While some couples have managed to create fantasy, intrigue, and mystery throughout the years, more have forgotten the games they used to play. As you've been reading, perhaps you've recalled some that you and your husband once shared. What were they? Take time to let them surface. Did you dress up like Scarlett and Rhett? Did you play the prince and the pauper? What did you say to each other when you were being fanciful? Did you talk about the future? When you were visualizing your lives together, weren't you making up the script, decorating the sets, choosing the costumes and the roles you wanted to play? Wasn't it a turn-on?

Consider what roles you'd like to play now. The advantage of a fantasy you can act out at home is that you never have to go public with it. No one but the two of you need know what you do behind closed doors. A secret is even more magical if it is shared when you are not alone: locking eyes and smiling slyly across a crowded room—at a party, meeting, or even parents' night at your kids' school—creates an atmosphere of mystery and intrigue between you. No matter which fantasy you choose, allow yourself the opportunity to fully enjoy it. If you can't think of a good fantasy—old or new—then read some erotica for inspiration.

The Flavor of an Office Romance

When people are having illicit love affairs they don't have to make up fantasies, they are living them. Their lives are filled with intrigue and tension. And many illicit affairs begin as office romances. We're not suggesting that you both find other lovers. We are suggesting an office affair between husband and wife—be in a secret relationship with your husband.

Could it work? Why not? For many people work is a most seductive lover. If you are married to a workaholic, what better way to share his addiction than to have an office romance with him? If you're the workaholic, an office affair will allow your husband to participate in your life in a new way. You will both see each other in different worlds, see new talents and skills not usually demonstrated at home. This fantasy allows both of you to experience each other much more fully. And, it will give you an opportunity to support each other, be on each other's teams in a new, more direct way. If neither of you is a workaholic, it will be just plain fun.

If you and your husband don't work together, you will have to develop a strategy with specific tactics to have an office romance with him. You will need to enlist his secretary as an ally—to make the dates for phone calls and lunches or meetings in unusual places, and as a go-between to create and maintain the distance you need for this fantasy.

Office affairs are conducted through phone conversations, lunch and drink dates, while traveling to and from the office, and during out-of-town meetings and conventions. Your illicit affair can follow the same pattern. Ask his secretary to put you on his calendar for a fifteen-minute phone conversation. When you have him on the line, pretend you aren't going to see him that night and talk about how much you enjoyed him that morning. Keep your voice low and sexy. Tell him you hope you can see him again, very soon. Play with him, even if he resists. Don't give up the way you might if this really were an illicit relationship. Keep the conversation light and flirtatious; end it by telling him that you love him. If he mentions your call that evening, pretend you don't know what he's talking about. Remember, you're embarking on an illicit relationship that only takes place during office hours and has no place at home! Repeat this tactic often, even if you feel silly. He'll begin to look forward to those calls; he may call you at your office to carry on the same sort of conversation.

Then, ask his secretary to schedule a lunch date for at least a week in advance. To keep the illusion of distance, don't make the date yourself. When he asks you what it's about, be mysterious, don't give him a reason, tell him only that you plan to be near his office and want to buy him lunch. Be sure to make a reservation at an intimate restaurant nearby. (If you aren't familiar with the neighborhood, call one of your single friends or ask his secretary.) Before you go to the table, make some arrangement with the maitre d' to ensure that you pay for the lunch and so you won't have to deal with money or a credit card at the table. Your husband will adore the idea that you took such care with the arrangements, especially if he's always the person who pays. At lunch pretend you are interviewing him for a magazine article about successful men. Ask him questions about his work you don't often ask or ask them in a new way. For example, you might ask him about the high point of his day or what he likes most about his work. You may think you know the answers, but if you really listen to him closely you may discover some new and surprising things about him.

On another day, perhaps when you're having your hair or nails done or you feel particularly good about yourself, call at the last minute and suggest lunch. If he's not free, don't be discouraged—keep trying until he is. When you arrive, step out of character if you must and flutter a bit. Fuss over him. Tell him how happy you are to be married to him. Knowing that he's made a woman happy is enormously gratifying to a man, so let him know it. Share something you've been meaning to tell him but never seem to remember when you're with him. Make a point of remembering those thoughts and mentioning them at lunch. One of the reasons office romances begin is that when people share common work, common goals, and common problems, they talk to each other frequently—they share feelings, ideas, successes, and failures. This is an opportunity for you to share your husband's work and for him to share yours. So use this time to find out about problems he's having and help him to find some solutions he may have overlooked. Find ways to share your insights so that he can really hear you, in the same way you'd share your insights with your own coworkers.

In general, use what you know to support your husband's

work. Use all those skills that are easy for you and harder for him. Pretend you're a coworker in his department and part of your job is to make his easier by providing what he's missing.

Molly knows that she is very gregarious and her husband is not. She finds it easy to meet people and talk to them no matter what their interests. Her husband is more formal and less able to make conversation to put others at ease. Over the years of her marriage Molly has gained more self-confidence and begun to notice that her ease with people makes a real difference in her husband's professional life. "I never thought being relaxed in a group was a special skill until I started going to business meetings with Al. But I realize now that it is not natural for most people—Al being one. When I became aware of it, I was able to provide support for Al at these meetings and not blame him because he seemed ill at ease. We've become a team. I chat with the clients, he handles their taxes. And frequently these days Al calls to let me know what's happened after his meetings. Our relationship is much fuller than I ever thought it could be. I feel like I'm a free-lance part of his office—it's very nice."

Once you've established the pattern of being in close touch during the workday, send flowers. Traditionally, married men have used flowers to atone for some error of judgment, breach of conduct, or because they forgot to buy a gift in time for an anniversary or birthday. What a shame that flowers aren't used more to demonstrate love and remembering. And, although the pattern is changing, most women do not send flowers to men, so a dozen roses delivered to his office on a Monday morning with a note saying,

"Good Morning" or "Thanks for the great weekend" or "Have a good day" is sure to be a pleasant surprise. Or send him an African violet with a note that says, "Every time I see a violet I think of that afternoon when we . . ." Or a terrarium with a note saying: "Watch the world go by with me."

"When Bob went off for a week of golf without me, I was unhappy and hurt," Barbara recalled. "He had won the trip because he was named Salesman of the Month, and it came at a time when I just couldn't get away. I'm afraid I turned my hurt into low-grade anger, and whenever I spoke to him I sounded cross and he sounded guilty. Clearly, he was not having as good a time as he should have been. Then I came to my senses and decided that as long as he was away, I wanted him to enjoy it. I called the hotel florist and arranged to have flowers sent to his room with a note that said, 'You score high with me. Keep your golf score low. I love you.'

"He came back two days early! He was very happy to see me and promised that he'd never consider taking a trip without me again. Since then I send flowers to his office at least once a month with notes saying things like, 'You've sold me' and 'You're my salesman of the month.' Bob loves it."

You can also send notes without flowers or put them in his briefcase or between the pages of important reports, as well as in his tennis bag or the pockets of his suits. Make them loving and sexy and explicit. You know what happens when you conjure up exotic and erotic pictures—you get turned on. And that is exactly what's supposed to happen: to you as you write the note, to him as he reads it. If you're embarrassed, start off simply with "I love you" or "I miss you." If you notice you're having difficulty being more explicit, try writing in the language you studied in school. Use a dictionary if you have to, but write the notes. Tell him what you liked about the last time you made love together; tell him what you're planning to do with him as soon as possible. And don't ask him if he's found the notes. Don't pout if he says nothing. Keep writing them.

Laura started writing notes to Michael when he moved to a new office. "I wanted him to feel good on his first day," she told us, "so I used a Post-it and put it on his calendar page. It said, 'I love you, you're the greatest.' I also put one in every one of his suit pockets so no matter which suit he chose he'd find one. Michael didn't acknowledge the notes that evening, and I felt a little peculiar. But the next morning when I opened my jewelry box, there was a note from him. That's how I knew he'd not only found them but loved them."

Next consider writing an old-fashioned love letter. Send it to the office marked "personal" because you don't really want anyone else to open it. Sign it "Your old girl friend." You'll be right. You were once. Remember?

After several weeks of phone calls, lunches, notes, and flowers, suggest that the two of you go home together at the end of the day. Suggest drinks before you get into the car, train, or bus. People having office affairs often have drinks together—why shouldn't you do the same? Use the time to flirt with him. Think of something unusual you saw or did that reminded you of him. Tell him. Ask him how he solved the problem he told you about at lunch. Become involved with his business concerns as well as his successes. Share your own. Ask his advice.

Meet him at his office (or yours) as often as possible so that the terrain will be familiar to both of you, just as it is when people are having illicit office romances. If you're having dinner with a couple you both enjoy, meet in the office before you join them. If you have financial matters to discuss, do it in the office, not at home. Expand your lives into your offices as much as feels appropriate. Susie told us that when she and Jake were having the painters, they slept in Jake's office one night. "Since Jake is a doctor, there are couches and bathrooms and a refrigerator. When Jake suggested sleeping there instead of going to a hotel, I thought he was crazy but I didn't argue. Actually, it turned into an exotic night. We both felt like we were someplace we shouldn't be—I couldn't shake the feeling that one of his nurses would show up and find us there. It was extremely titillating, and we had great sex! We've gone back there to sleep several times since the painters finished their work. No one knows we're there. It's both a great escape and exciting."

How far are you willing to go in your office romance? Will you go as far as Louise? "I wanted to do something special for Mark's birthday—something that would simply stagger him. So I called his secretary and asked her to schedule a meeting for him with a prospective client at a hotel near his office. His secretary and I made up a name and a company, and I checked into the hotel under that name. I was terrified. I'd never done anything like that. In fact, I was anxious every minute of the way. I was so afraid we'd get our signals crossed or that his secretary hadn't really told him or he'd be suspicious. And I kept thinking the hotel detective would find out I'd used an assumed name. But that only heightened my excitement. By the time Mark knocked on the door and I opened it wearing the sheerest, sexiest teddy I could find, I was trembling. His first look was shock; then he grinned from ear to ear, even though he was speechless. We spent the afternoon surrounded by pillows and blankets in a huge bed, drinking champagne, giggling, and feeling madly in love. Mark said it was the best birthday present I could have given him—especially since it was so out of character, so outrageous. I'll have to really work to come up with another birthday surprise as exciting as that one.''

In spite of her anxiety and embarrassment, Louise created a superb fantasy and then acted it out. It had all the ingredients inherent in romantic moments: the unexpected, tension, surprise, uncertainty, the illicit, a bit of terror, eroticism, and ultimately, consummation. Louise and Mark also share a new element of mystery—he can never be sure that she won't surprise him again. He can't read her mind as well as he thought he could and the ordinary turned into the extraordinary. Louise's afternoon was a perfect way to conduct an office romance.

Having an office romance with your husband never has to take place at home. You can keep pretending that you don't know what he's talking about when he mentions the note in his diary or the flowers or the phone calls. Or you can choose to make it an obvious part of your life together and let everyone know. Since it's your fantasy, you can create it at any time. And enjoy it.

Other Fantasies

If you or your husband travel for work, you have some other exotic options. Airports, train stations, or other busy public places are ideal settings for making believe and creating fantasies. You can pretend you've just met, you can pick each other up. If you're lucky, you might be able to meet him in cities you might not otherwise visit together. There, you can pretend that no one knows where you are or that you really have moved to a new place.

"One of the best parts of traveling on my job," according to Glenna, "is that every now and then Henry and I can arrange a rendezvous. We have met in some wonderful hotels in other cities. We had a terrific time at the Ritz Carlton in Chicago when Henry was there on business and so was I. It's true that even before I got there, I was worried about the hotel arrangements. Since he had been staying at the Ritz and I was joining him, I was worried that the people at the registration desk wouldn't be expecting me or perhaps they wouldn't believe that I was his wife, or they'd think I was only there to check up on him. It's amazing how our minds come up with all these incredible things when we're uncomfortable about what we're doing. After I was safely in the room I couldn't imagine why the people at the desk would even care, as long as the room was paid for! On the other hand, for the time it took the clerks to locate all the papers I became damp with fear and, at the same time, felt titillated and excited.

"By the time I got to the room, I had convinced myself that I was the illicit guest I'd imagined the clerk thought I was! I was exactly in the right mood for a love affair."

* * *

If you can't arrange a rendezvous in a different city, use the advantages inherent in separations: a short time apart allows both of you some freedom to see people you don't see together or spend time alone with your children or clean out your closets. It also allows you the opportunity to have late-night phone conversations when both of you are in bed in different cities. You can anticipate what will happen when the two of you are together again. You can tease and flirt as you might have done before you were married. You can send flowers to his room or arrange for a midnight snack you usually eat together then, and you can certainly put love notes in his luggage, his toilet kit, his briefcase, even in his shoes.

These attentions can pave the way for your husband to share, once again, his fantasies with you. Together the two of you can expand and explore a new and exciting terrain. Perhaps you will create a secret code, like Nina and Leonard. He will know if you leave a message with his secretary that says "Don't forget to bring home cat food," it really means "I can't wait to get you into bed tonight." Or his message to you is "I've made the travel arrangements," and you'll know it means "I've been thinking all day about our sexy conversations on airplanes."

Routines and regularity are part of enduring relationships. Spice them with intrigue—"Meet me at the supermarket at six, I've got a surprise for you." Lighten them with games—"We're hardly ever home for dinner together so when we are, let's pretend we have to keep it a secret." Heighten them with mystery—you make it up.

10

Having a Love Affair With Your Husband

Perfect Vacations—Are They Possible?

Now you are having a love affair with your husband. You feel splendid. So does he. You've lost some weight or changed your hairstyle and makeup or reassessed your wardrobe. There is a lightness in your step and every inch of your body feels sleek, lithe, and well loved. You love the way you look. You love the way he looks even more. You can tell how good he feels by his boyish grin and the twinkle in his eye and the lilt in his voice. It's as if you two had just met; yet your relationship is more profound and much more satisfying. Each day brings a new and surprising delight, an unexpected gesture—each of you sends the other three yellow roses that arrive simultaneously though you haven't consulted each other and neither has ever done this before. Each night is loving and sensuous—whether or not you choose to make love, it feels as though you caress each other with your eyes and your voices. Old routines have been energized—you are more brilliant at work, more scintillating at parties, more patient and sage with your children, and your mother-in-law has told you how smart her son was to have chosen you. You love being together and when you are apart, you make plans for a vacation that will allow you to escape everything, to hide away and indulge your deepest sensual desires.

You and your husband are in your brand-new red sports car. The top is down and the wind whips through your hair. You feel as free as you did when you'd just met. The two of you are sitting as close together as the gear shift allows, exhilarated to be on your way, alone with each other. The scenery as you drive up the coast encompasses ocean views and endless turnpikes and you love both. You take your time getting to the boat. Since you're not in a hurry, you stop at a crafts fair, pick wildflowers along the side of the road, and eat when you're hungry. Behind you is work, the children, your everyday life. As you get closer to the sea, the salt air makes you want to go a little faster so you can begin your ten-day sail. You board at low tide, climbing down a twenty-foot ladder to the dinghy below. You step into the little boat. As you watch him board, you feel that life is just right and always will be. The days on the sailboat have a different pace, one you hadn't imagined. You get up early to ready the boat for the day's sail. Getting the sails up, moving speedily out of the harbor, you are both totally enraptured. You see each other in new ways. You like what you see. Your bodies feel different, more in sync with each other and the world around you. As the day warms, your body glows. So does his. The afternoons have a slower pace. You read or take turns at the helm. You anchor each evening in a new place—Christmas Cove, Bass Harbor, Northeast Harbor, Seal Bay—each one is different, each is special. Some nights you eat on board and listen to tapes you found on the boat. Some nights you try the inns or cafes in the harbor. Then you slip into each other's arms and into a perfect sleep, exhausted from the sea and sun. You are utterly content. You came away together with no preconceived ideas of what this vacation would be like, so there is nothing with which to compare it. It's perfect just the way it is.

And then you remember all your past perfectly planned holidays that did not live up to expectations. In fact, you remember how awful they were, and how you couldn't wait to escape back home. How does one ever go on a vacation and have it be perfect? How in the world can one plan a holiday as part of this love affair and have it work out?

"When we had been married for about ten years," Risa told us, "I admitted it—our vacations never turned out the way we wanted them to and one of us was always disappointed. Either it rained in the Caribbean or there was no snow in Vermont or the car broke down or someone got sick and we couldn't leave or we missed the plane or we hated the hotel or spent more money than we had planned. The first few years I thought it was his fault—he wanted to go skiing—or my fault—I picked the hotel. Or we were jinxed and the weather was deliberately uncooperative. One day I was complaining about vacations to some friends and found they'd all had very similar experiences. I realized that all vacations have at least one thing in common: they never match our expectations. Never."

We think Risa is right. Vacations are often doomed before they begin because they are based on images of perfection and visions found only in TV commercials, both of which are unrealistic. The chances that anyone will romp in a calm sea, do a perfect slalom down a pristine slope, or nestle cozily, undisturbed in front of a blazing hearth, are slim. In truth, the opportunity for disappointment abounds; satisfaction and elation are elusive.

"I discovered our solution during the worst possible start of a holiday," Marcy told us. "We were booked on a first-class flight to Martinique the week before Christmas. We arrived at the airport about ten minutes before flight time to find we were among fifty people who had been bounced. The flight had been overbooked. The airline offered every possible concession including two first-class tickets to any-where in the world but my husband wasn't having any of it. He was furious. Although I was just as upset, I was also embarrassed until I noticed that the other fifty people were clustered around him. He had become their spokesman (even if they were willing to take the other tickets). Still, we did not get on that plane although our luggage did. We booked a morning flight and left the airport. It was a hideous night, cold and damp with a bone-chilling rain. We were dressed for the tropics. On our way back to the apartment I had a brainstorm. I reminded Dave that since everyone thought we were en route, no one would know where we were. We could do anything we wanted that night. After all, our vacation had begun even though we hadn't left town. I called a favorite restaurant, told them to chill a bottle of champagne, and we went for dinner. The maitre d' asked what we were celebrating. Dave told him, 'Turning a disaster into a party.' A party we continued after we got home. We left for Martinique the next day feeling terribly pleased with ourselves because we had turned a big upset in our plans into a great time."

"How did that experience become a solution for other holidays?" we asked.

"I've stopped thinking that a vacation has to be perfect to be fun. Because the trip to Martinique began with a disaster, I couldn't pretend that the situation was great. It was clear that we had to do something drastic so we could recapture our holiday mood. I realized that I had made a permanent, though unwritten, list of vacation spoilers. Anytime any one of those spoilers popped up, and one always did, then the vacation was doomed. Since I've realized it's possible to have fun no matter what, I no longer have to hold on to my fantasy of the 'perfect' vacation. Now as part of my planning, I make a list of things that could go wrong. I actually write down all the things I can think of—usually well in advance, sometimes in the cab on the way to the airport. So when we went to Paris for the first time, and it rained five of the seven days we were there, neither of us got too upset. I had put bad weather on my list. I'm not going to tell you we loved having wet feet, ruining at least two pairs of shoes, and carrying umbrellas everywhere. But do you know how beautiful Paris is in the rain? It's a painting by Utrillo come to life. And warming up in the oversized bathtub in our oversized bathroom was a wonderful way to make ourselves feel pampered. I hope I don't sound like Pollyanna. It's just that I finally realized that we weren't going to cancel a trip just because of rain, so there's no point complaining about it. No matter where you go there are lots of things to enjoy anyway."

Marcy and Dave have discovered the principle of "inclusion." Included in their vacation plans are all the things that can go wrong and often do. As a result, when it rains or a plane takes off without them or the hotel can't find their reservations or they get lost or their bags do, it doesn't mean the end of a good time or the loss of a perfect holiday. The possibility has been included in the plan. Clearly, rain in Paris or the Caribbean is not, in itself, a holiday spoiler; it is just one of the weather variables of those (and most) parts of the world.

It is *how* you react to the rain that spoils the vacation. And, indeed, a missed plane can be the start of an adventure if you include it and use it to your own advantage as Risa and Dave did. Howard and Ann used a different holiday spoiler as the start of their adventure.

When we asked them to tell us about their best vacation, they told us about their first (and last) cruise. "We quickly discovered that no medication in the world was going to cure my mal de mer," Howard said. "I had to face it. I'm a terrible sailor, and I hated every moment on the boat. I felt guilty for spoiling Ann's vacation, but I was too sick to care about the gala activities and the deluxe accommodations."

"It's true," Ann added. "He was the worst sailor. I tried to be gallant, but I wasn't happy about it at all. Finally, in desperation, we decided to get off at the next port, which was Morocco. Our relief to be on land was soon replaced by apprehension as we realized we knew nothing about where we were."

"We drove in a state of silent terror from the port city to Marakesh, the only place we had ever heard of in Morocco. I kept thinking 'What if we get sick, get lost, get robbed,'" Howard continued. "We didn't say anything to each other until we were safely in the hotel. Then we realized we were in the middle of the adventure of our lives. Once we stopped listening to our racing thoughts, we were able to enjoy being in Morocco on a fantastic, unplanned holiday where everything we did was new and different and unexpected. It was terrific."

Ann's and Howard's trip could have turned into a disaster had they not been willing to take positive advantage of their circumstances. Without realizing it, they were operating according to the principle of inclusion. You can, too.

All-Inclusive Vacation Planner

As you daydream about your second or third honeymoon, include in your plans all the things that might go wrong along with everything that could be just right. Before you make real plans, practice. Imagine that you've won an all-expense-paid vacation to Paris, city of light and romance. There are round-trip tickets for the Concorde, a suite at the Hotel Crillon where the walls are hung with silk and the linen bedsheets are changed every day. Perfect meals at two- and three-star restaurants have been ordered and paid for in advance. An extravagant shopping allowance is part of the prize. The only requirement is that you submit a list of everything that might spoil this perfect holiday. You must include every possible problem so start at the very beginning. Think of all the things that could go wrong immediately.

Do you have to make special arrangements for taking off time from work or do you have some vacation left? Will you have to work extra hard before or after the holiday? Will your husband? How do you feel about that? Do you have to make arrangements for the kids? For the dog? Do you have a list of trustworthy sitters or will you have to find one?

Next, consider what clothes to take. Do you have the right ones? If not, do you have the time to shop? Do you have enough money? Do you have the proper luggage? Can you get it? What else could be a problem for you? Are you afraid of flying? Is your husband? What if the sitter cancels at the last minute? Can you call your mother or is she unable to leave her job on short notice?

Keep thinking of all the things that could go wrong for you or your husband. Is packing a problem for you or for him? Do you always forget to buy something—something that might cause an argument between you? What about getting to the airport? Are you afraid you'll get caught in traffic? Are you always anxious about missing flights while your husband seems to have a cavalier attitude about timing and schedules? Does this cause tension between you? Is one of you a worrier and the other so relaxed that you can't stand each other at these moments? If you acknowledged this, you could act beforehand to alleviate it as a source of tension.

In this particular game plan you get to the airport on time and the plane takes off on schedule. You arrive in Paris three hours later full of the best champagne and caviar Air France has to offer. Once there, however, new problems can arise. In Paris they speak French. Do you? If not, how will you both deal with the uncertainty of being in a new and strange place? Did one of you remember to take a phrase book or will you have to struggle when you want to change dollars into francs? What will it feel like not being able to understand what people are saying, not knowing where the hotel is or how much the cab should cost? Will you two remain calm or could this be a flash point for you? Has this sort of disagreement spoiled your vacations in the past? You can avoid it this time by preparing for it, and "including" it.

Now, picture yourselves arriving at the hotel. Did you bring the reservations? Do you like your suite or is it too small, too large and impersonal, without a view, on too low a floor? Are the beds too soft, too hard, too narrow? So many things may have gone wrong by now that you could be feeling miserable, in danger of wanting to turn around and go home. Or you could go out and walk around the Place de la Concorde. Paris is beautiful and you are both thrilled to be there—until it starts to rain. Did you bring a raincoat and an umbrella? Are you going to allow your first trip to Paris to be spoiled by rain? Are you suddenly sorry you didn't win a trip to Aruba instead? And if you did win the trip to Aruba, what would have spoiled that holiday?

The point, of course, is that things do go wrong and, while calling attention to them can be discouraging, being aware can make a big difference. Knowing in advance what to expect is very liberating. Just as you and your husband have made unspoken agreements about what you can and can't do in your own home, you've made unspoken agreements about your vacations. Acknowledging those unspoken agreements and expectations allows you to change them and make new ones. Start out with the intention of creating a new freedom for yourselves—the freedom to have a great vacation no matter what comes up. Make your list of vacation spoilers and share it with your husband. Let him add his own disasters. The longer the list grows, the funnier it will be. The list will serve as an insurance policy —because at least three are sure to occur during any vacation and when they do, you'll be prepared to laugh and keep going instead of letting them stop you as you may have done in the past. By the time you've taken three vacations using this system, you'll be an expert in vacation planning and probably won't need the list ever again.

Fantasy Weekends

The best vacations occur when two people have the same expectations. If one of you has a vision of languorous days and sensual nights and the other expects to be an excellent tour guide, both of you are going to be disappointed. And if one of you feels out of control and anxious in a strange place, some childish patterns of behavior are likely to surface. These, unfortunately, can defeat the purpose of the vacation. Before you plan a fantasy weekend, find out what your husband's fantasy is. Unless he has just described it to you, don't assume you know. You can experiment by arranging to be alone, together, right at home. You will have to organize this in advance, but you can do it on a low budget and minimize your risk. Make arrangements for your children to be elsewhere—at their friend's or a grandparent's house; stock your refrigerator with your favorite foods and plan to ignore the telephone.

"Have you ever spent a great weekend alone in your own home?" we asked Peggy.

"Yes. Recently, our two older children were away on a

school trip, and then the youngest was invited to sleep at a friend's. We were so excited by the prospect of being alone right at home—I can't remember when we had been since the kids were born—that we decided to make do with whatever was in the house and not worry about shopping for anything, not even the Sunday papers. We took a bath together and made love with the doors open and all the lights on and the TV blaring. We felt as energized and refreshed as if we'd spent a fortune on a vacation at a health spa. When the kids came home on Sunday night they could sense that something was different, but being self-centered as kids are, they thought it had something to do with them. They decided we'd gone Christmas shopping, and searched the house for hidden presents. We looked at each other and laughed."

Peggy's and Richard's unexpected weekend was like a bonus but gave them no time to plan ahead. If you do choose a weekend in advance, one way to keep things spontaneous is to divide up the planning so that neither of you knows all the arrangements. Ask your husband to plan one of the meals. If he doesn't cook, he can have something delivered or choose a restaurant. If you choose the restaurant, pay the check in advance so that he feels like he's being taken out—even if he'll get the credit card bill later. Arrange to see a movie that is guaranteed to turn you on. Buy an erotic book and read it aloud. Have a picnic in the living room, give each other a massage in the dining room. Have the newspapers delivered (if you care) and agree that neither of you will do any work for two days.

Planning a weekend that doesn't cost much but that emphasizes privacy and togetherness in a sexy way requires only a little ingenuity and perhaps a small flair for the dramatic. It is fun to step out of character from time to time, and you needn't be concerned that you will become a card-carrying pornographer in danger of losing your respectability or Gloria Steinem's approval. Besides, no one will know but the two of you.

Exchanging homes with a friend or relative is another inexpensive way to have a fantasy weekend. It's best if the other couple lives in a different environment from your own. Ginny lives in a rural part of Connecticut and her sister Mimi lives in the middle of Manhattan. When they swapped homes for a weekend, each organized her home so that the other couple could spend the two days entirely as guests—everything was attended to beforehand. Each sister created a fantasy for the other to step into.

Ginny made plans emphasizing the best of country life: There was enough wood stacked near the fireplace to last for two days, a bowl of fresh apples in the bedroom, and a stewpot simmering on the stove in her big country kitchen. She left notes directing Mimi and her husband to special treats—a walk through the woods that led, like a treasure hunt, to another note that told where the cocoa and mulled wine were. Ginny had even turned off the phone so that the spell of being secluded in the country would not be broken.

In Mimi's apartment Ginny and her husband found notes and special touches highlighting life in the big city. Chilled champagne and elegant hors d'oeuvres were set in exactly the right spot for watching the sun set over Manhattan. There was a special movie already in the VCR; there were bath salts and a new massage oil in the bathroom and scented candles in the bedroom. Reservations had been made for Saturday evening at a popular new restaurant, and an elegant brunch was delivered on Sunday morning.

Each couple discovered that there is something illicit about being in someone else's house and bed. When they were in each other's homes both Ginny and Mimi were surprised to feel a slightly secretive sensation that enhanced their pleasure. (If cost is not a problem, exchange space with a friend who lives in another part of the country.)

If you can't fit a weekend alone into your schedule in the near future, then plan an afternoon together doing something you don't usually do. Go to a museum or an afternoon concert, take a picnic to a nearby park, rent a room in a local hotel, or meet at home for lunch (if you're sure no one else will be there). Or turn one of those boring automobile trips we all have to make from time to time into something more exciting.

Betty and Mark have a weekend house in the country that is a two-hour drive away. A slight shift in perspective has changed that boring trip for them both: they realized that those two hours are often the only time they can be alone—no phone, no guests, no children, no work. They now use that time to talk, to plan together, to play "remember when," and to explore ways to enhance their affair of twenty-five years.

Having a Great Vacation—
No Matter What

Planning a vacation that costs money raises questions not just about the nature of the vacation, but how much you want to spend on it. Do you know how you feel about spending money on yourself? How does your husband feel?

Since we rarely know exactly what the other's assumptions are (we barely know our own), how and where to spend money on vacations often creates more problems than the vacation may solve—or so it seems.

Think of a time you were on a holiday that turned into a disaster. Where were you? Who were you with? Was it an expensive vacation? What did you expect to happen? What did your husband expect? What did you each do when you realized that the holiday was not fitting the image you'd had of it? What did you want to do about it? Why didn't you? What would have happened if you had? What decision did you make about vacations as a result? Are you still operating from that decision? Isn't it time to make some new decisions?

Think of the conversations you have had with your husband about "the perfect vacation." If you were planning a holiday just to please him, what would it be? How expensive would it be? How different is your version of the ideal vacation? Is there any way you can make the two ideals mesh?

Liz thinks the perfect vacation is camping in the woods. Her husband, Eric, thinks it's an elegant country inn with antiques in every room and gourmet food. "After years of doing one or the other," Liz told us, "we planned a weekend so we could do both—one night of camping, the next in Eric's favorite inn. It was great. We both felt satisfied, and on the way home we decided when we were going to do it again. Neither felt resentful this time that we were giving in to the other. I suspect we could go back to one kind of trip or the other now that we've both extended ourselves during the same weekend. We got our pâté and campfire marshmallows, too."

*   *   *

Whether you have lots of money and don't need to win a prize to fly on the Concorde or you have an extremely small vacation budget and can't imagine going off by your selves until the kids have graduated from college, taking time off—just the two of you—is essential. It recharges your bodies, your psyches, and your love affair. So send your kids off for the weekend, swap houses, add a few days to a business trip, sneak off when you make the obligatory visit to your mother or his—no matter where she lives. Search the pages of travel magazines that are within your budget and have a love affair with your husband.

11

Follow-up
and Follow-through

You're having a love affair with your husband because you've decided that there is no other way to live. You can remember the moment you made that decision and how empowering it was. Now, you notice the difference it makes in your life—how much more fun it is, how much easier it is to get over annoyances and upsets. You've discovered your own power and used it to lift your marriage out of the ordinary. You've created access to your own passion and sensuality. You've seen the possibilities in commitment—its emphasis on exploration and development as individuals as well as a couple. Somehow, the clearer you are about your commitment and the appropriateness of your relationship, the richer and more varied it becomes. And as it grows, so do the two of you.

During the course of our research, we discussed marriage with many people. We began to see how those marriages that are ongoing love affairs differ from those that are simply enduring marriages. We observed a difference similar to the one between a smashing Broadway success and a conscientious workmanlike staging. People engaged in workmanlike performances are not fully accessing their potential. They settle for less. Enduring marriages that aren't love affairs can have many satisfactions—security, comfort, and companionship; these are certainly rare and wonderful qualities. But the couples who aren't experiencing a love affair in their marriage are settling for less. People in these relationships hold back a part of themselves. They're unwilling to risk giving all. They may repress their anger—because it frightens them or because they believe it is inappropriate; they may withhold their total support—because they fear it will be rejected. They may be holding back a part of themselves because they're unsure how they've changed and don't know they have even more to give now.

We're not going to pretend that letting go of what you are withholding is easy. Or that accessing your best or facing some risk is always fun. It's not. It requires hard work. You have to become adept at seeing yourself and your behavior clearly—to become more aware of yourself; to notice what you're doing and not make judgments about your actions and not blame someone else either; to observe yourself, collect information, absorb it, process it, and allow yourself to take a new point of view.

We noted some constants among people who describe their marriages as love affairs. They have a clear sense of their own identities—separate from their partners—a tolerance of their partner's behavior, the ability to forgive them selves as well as the other person, a willingness to be responsible for their own anger and resentments.

"I know I'm having a love affair with my husband," Lizzie told us, "because he's the one I want to be with the most, and our views on the important issues of life are always the same, no matter how they might differ on the smaller ones. But it's odd, I never expected to be as independent as I am; his work and school schedule leave me no choice. I've had to build a life for myself. Nevertheless, I think it's been very good for us. My independence allows me to know I'm choosing him all the time."

People who describe their marriages as love affairs are long on tolerance. They are willing to allow the other person to be exactly who he or she is, to behave the way he or she behaves.

"Sure," Pamela admitted. "Sometimes I wish that Richie was less sensitive and didn't have such a quick temper. But then suddenly I'll see him from a distance and feel a flood of affection and love for him, and then I'll remember that those characteristics are part of why I love him so much."

The difference between a marriage that is also a love affair and a marriage that is "just" solid can be illustrated by the ways two women—both of whom love their husbands—handled the same problem: their husbands were fired from well-paying executive positions. Sheila had no illusions about job security and was well aware of the stresses of corporate life. Her awareness made it easy for her to be concerned for Scott's well-being without feeling threatened herself. Karen was angry at her husband and assumed he could have done something different in order to save his job because she has never been consciously aware of how she feels about being dependent on Ed's salary. But Karen was unwilling to acknowledge her anger because she believed it was inappropriate. Since she did not deal with her rage it festered, sabotaging her commitment to her husband and her marriage. Since Karen does love Ed, she can't allow herself to openly berate him for being fired. Instead, her anger simmers below the surface. It is not truly acknowledged, ever, so that it can't dissipate, ever. It rarely explodes, it's just there. It prevents her from fully appreciating the man she chose to marry. Karen's unawareness of her own reactions to the loss of security as well as the unexamined decision that her anger would be misplaced here, interferes with her ability to be a supportive partner.

We talked to many women like Karen who love their husbands deeply but do not think of themselves as having love affairs. They are engaged in relationships that we call "near misses." They hold back and so are unable to be as vulnerable as is necessary to have a love affair. They haven't taken responsibility for choosing their relationship in the first place or for making an ongoing commitment to make it the best they can.

Grace feels she comes second—second to her husband's business obligations, second to his children from his first marriage. She doesn't realize it is she, not Herb, who has set this up. Grace anticipates Herb's every move from this perspective and thinks it's dangerous to admit her hurt feelings. Instead, she withholds her feelings and expresses her unhappiness through petty criticism.

Grace has forgotten the love affair she and Herb were having before they got married. She has forgotten that in those days all his concerns were hers, and she felt she came first in his life. The complications were present then but they didn't matter. In fact, Grace thought his concern for everything, and everyone, in his life was a wonderful attribute. Nevertheless, now Grace's picture of "wife" doesn't match her circumstances—and the man who was the perfect lover turns out to be a less-than-perfect husband.

You cannot have a successful, fulfilling, ongoing, long-lasting love affair with someone whose behavior and style you intend to change. (Not that we all don't try from time to time.) No matter how compliant a person may be at the beginning of a relationship (after all, at the start aren't we all on our best behavior?), no matter how in love with you he is, eventually your attempts will seem intrusive, critical, and worse, rejecting. On the other hand, remembering what was wonderful, what works, what is thrilling, and acting upon it enables you to change your image of the perfect lover to fit the man you love. As Pamela does, when she talks about Richie.

We saw, time and time again, the power and pleasure inherent in remembering how love affairs began. When Jim described how the sunlight glinted in the hair of his wife-to-be the first afternoon they met, his eyes sparkled. When Don told us he knew he'd marry Angela as soon as she opened the door, he was clearly reliving that moment. If Grace remembered and behaved again as she did when she first met Herb, the change in her demeanor would remind him that they were having a love affair, once. Joy is catching. Justine Sterling, therapist, marriage counselor, and Director of the Sterling Institute, an organization committed to transforming the quality of people's relationships, maintains in his workshops that "knowing he's made a woman happy is enormously gratifying to a man. It makes him feel good."

Grace might find it difficult to explore which of the routines of her marriage to Herb can be altered. She'd have to give up the familiar, if unsatisfactory, routine and create a new, more rewarding one. She'd have to be willing to move a few steps to the right or left in order to gain a new perspective on her marriage. Instead, she feels hurt and angry.

Sadly, the impact of anger seems much stronger than that of affection, fondness, or even passionate love. Anger leaves scars because we don't seem able to view it as just another human emotion or accept arguing as just another natural normal activity. In fact, if people didn't get angry, fight, and make up, there'd be nothing with which to compare the good times. Life would have a sameness about it —there'd be no contrasts. It might become very boring to be happy all the time. (How would you know you were happy?) What makes anger so dangerous is the scars it can leave. Words are never carved in stone unless some action is taken. Even then actions resulting from anger can be reversed if both people agree. Anger, rages, quarrels, fits of temper don't have to mean very much in the end if the combatants understand that those feelings are simply part of the whole range of human emotions.

Sally and George know that their bickering is part of their relationship. Indeed, it is part of how they make love. They enjoy the fights because they enjoy making up. Incorporating fighting into their lives acknowledges anger as a human foible. After all, no one person can ever say "the right thing" all the time. In any enduring relationship, both people will inevitably say and do the wrong things from time to time. So what? Those words and actions only count against you if you say they do. And are the angry words really more important than how much you love each other or how good you can make each other feel?

(If you do feel you're in an intolerable relationship, we are not suggesting that you grin and bear it. If you cannot deal with the quarrels you have with your husband, if you and he engage in truly damaging arguments, get some counseling. In the end not all marriages can be saved. But this book is not about those relationships.)

For our research we talked to men as well as women. Many of these men love their wives deeply, but do not describe their marriages as love affairs—although they'd like to be able to. We asked them to describe what element was missing from their otherwise satisfying relationships.

"If only she'd cook breakfast for me once or twice a year," Lawrence confessed, "I'd be thrilled. I've always loved breakfast. Before I got married, I had visions of my wife getting up early and serving wonderful breakfasts. I could not wait to get home from our honeymoon to eat the pancakes and bacon and eggs and toast and coffee. But my wife is an oversleeper who couldn't care less about breakfast. So I've been making it for twenty years. If she'd only get up early from time to time and do it for me, well . . ." Lawrence's eyes got misty and he stopped in midsentence. We wanted to call his wife immediately! Clearly she doesn't realize how little it would take to make her marriage more satisfying—it would be a step in the direction of elevating it from workmanlike to a smashing success and a love affair. That relatively insignificant gesture would please Larry so thoroughly that he'd probably turn himself inside out to please his wife for months afterward.

As a barometer of your relationship, recall what therapists and marriage counselors Judith and Robert Shaw said about the "secondary thoughts" people have about their relationships: "People in good marriages don't give much weight to their secondary thoughts [he doesn't hug me enough; I don't like taking out the garbage all the time], people in unsatisfactory marriages pay a lot of attention to those thoughts, give them weight and meaning until they become more important than the relationship. And then they get divorced." They cannot incorporate into their marriages the foibles of their mates.

As we discovered, men and women who call their marriages love affairs were eager to talk about them.

"I don't mind talking about my marriage," William told us. "Talking about the good times makes it feel as if they were happening again. Ruth and I have been married for fifty-one years! And I still love her as much as I did when I married her. You want to know what made it possible? Well, I think it's being able to accept the other person, being willing to be there for them no matter what happens. When people know that, it makes it easier for them to get over the bad times and on with the good."

Judith has been married for forty-one years. "Flexibility. That's what makes it possible. Of course, you have to be able to talk to each other, to communicate. But if you love each other, flexibility is the key."

"You know, Steve and I both forgot our eighth anniversary this year," Lynn told us, "and realized at the same instant that we'd forgotten. And it didn't matter at all. We both laughed and went on with our day. But that spontaneous understanding between us is very precious. It allows us to feel secure and committed and to achieve that sense of well-being so vital to having a love affair."

"Everything has two sides to it," Janet began. "When everything is predictable it's boring. Yet, I love the familiarity and dependability of our marriage. We never seem to agree on how to spend money for extravagant things. At the same time we're in total agreement about everything that is truly important. When I'm irritated or angry or upset, I seem to notice only the negatives. I completely forget the good things. In fact, when I'm upset, there isn't any other way. I wonder how long it will take me, how many years of marriage, before I realize that's what I always do? And then I get over it."

"Yes. Definitely. Martin and I are having a love affair," Joan said. "But not every minute, not every day, not even every month. There's an ebb and flow in our relationship. Sometimes our passion for each other is intense and lasts for months; and then weeks will go by without either one of us wanting to make love. But we're still best friends. On the other hand, there are days when I think I hate him, but I'd never want to leave him or him to leave me. This relationship is 'it' for us. Neither of us would have it any other way."

No one can feel as if they are having a love affair all the time, not even people who are having love affairs and aren't married. So when having a love affair with your husband begins to feel like work, don't. And don't worry about it. Do remember that you were having one last night, last week, last month, and you will again. Don't blame yourself, don't blame him. Relax and enjoy the relationship you have.

Among the dictionary definitions of "commitment" is "an agreement or pledge to do something in the future."

You are committed to the man you married. You are committed to your love for him. You are committed to your future together. You are committed to having a love affair with him before someone else does. And you are.

Epilogue:
Reflections on Success

A love affair begins when two people are willing to fall
in love. It begins when two people are willing to choose
each other for a love affair. Probably they could have chosen many other people, but they didn't. They chose each
other. Having a love affair with your husband is really no
different. It begins with a willingness to fall in love, all over
again, and a willingness to choose him for romance, again.
Having a love affair with your husband begins as a state of
mind and continues as a result of choosing, every day, that
he is the one with whom you are willing to have a love
affair. It requires a state of mind in which both of you are
willing to acknowledge your commitment to each other, to
nourish that commitment so that it can flourish. That com-

mitment becomes like an umbrella under which everything—every joy, disappointment, rage, upset, contentment—is protected and included. It is a powerful force that allows both of you to forgive, forget, fulfill, and flourish together. From time to time you both may feel a little damp around the edges yet the core of your relationship remains safe and dry. Still, the umbrella of commitment has to be created and re-created again and again. It cannot be taken for granted. If it is, it will blow away.

Enduring love affairs, ones that allow two people to grow and change and expand, only occur when each person has a clear sense of self, separate from the other, and a sense that together they create another third self, a self that is their marriage. The third self becomes a reference point, a home base, a cozy corner, a launching pad, a flexible structure that can accommodate the good and the bad—no matter what. Marriages that are also enduring love affairs happen between two people who aren't stuck in old outdated patterns, people who are willing to examine their points of view, to reflect on nonproductive actions and thoughts, to shift and change when it is appropriate in order to preserve that third self that is their marriage.

"I've been married for almost forty years," one woman told us, "and it gets better all the time. There is a way of caring about someone with whom you've shared your whole life that is unimaginable until you get there. But it's so worth getting there."

This woman in her sixties looks like every other woman in the middle of a love affair—she is vital and excited; she sparkles and glows with well-being. Clearly, anyone who has been with the same man for so many years and who continues to express so much joy about her marriage is, indeed, having a love affair with her husband.

And you can, too.

...gush his business concerns as well as his successes. Share your own. Ask his advice.

Selected Bibliography

Chapter One

1. Tim Gallwey, *Inner Tennis: Playing the Game* (New York: Random House, 1976), pp. 47–48.
2. Robert C. Solomon, *Love: Emotion, Myth and Metaphor* (Garden City, N.Y.: Doubleday/Anchor, 1981), p. 48.

Chapter Two

1. Alexandra Penney, *Great Sex* (New York: William Morrow, 1985).
2. Interview, May 1985, Robert Shaw, M.D., Judith Shaw, M. S., Co-Directors, Family Institute, Berkeley, Calif.
3. Solomon, *Love,* p. 146.
4. Gallwey, *Inner Tennis,* p. 57.

Chapter Three

Group interview, March 1985, New York.

Chapter Four

1. Willard Gaylor, *The Rage Within, Anger in Modern Life* (New York: Simon & Schuster, 1984), pp. 90–91.
2. Group interview, November 1985, New York.

Chapter Five

1. Gallwey, *Inner Tennis.*
2. David Bodonis, *The Body Book: A Fantastic Voyage to the World Within* (Boston: Little, Brown, 1984).

3. Robert Rivlin and Karen Gravelle, *Deciphering the Senses* (New York: Simon & Schuster, 1984), p. 40.

Chapter Six

1. Carole Jackson, *Color Me Beautiful* (New York: Ballantine Books, 1982).
2. Robert Ponti, *Dressing to Win* (New York: Doubleday, 1984)
3. Mark Knapp, Robert Hopper, Robert Bell, "The Fine Art of Compliments," *Psychology Today* (August 1985), pp. 25–28.

Chapter Seven

1. Trevanian, *Shibumi* (New York: Crown Publishers, Inc., 1979).

Chapter Eight

1. Dr. Sy Silverberg, unpublished study on parameters of "normal" sexual behavior, "The Normal Dilemma," The Canadian Institute for Sex Research, (Sept. 1984).
2. Carol Botwin, *Is There Sex After Marriage?* (Boston: Little, Brown, 1985), p. 22.
3. Alexandra Penney, *Great Sex* (New York: William Morrow, 1985), p. 191.
4. Daniel Goleman, "New Studies Examine Sexual Guilt," *The New York Times* (September 22, 1985).

Chapter Nine

1. Anne-Marie Villefranche, *Joie d' Amour, An Erotic Memoir of Paris in the 1920's* (New York: Carroll & Graf, 1984). Translated by Jane Purcell.
2. Solomon, *Love*, p. 49.

Chapter Eleven

1. Interview, April 1986, Justine, Sterling, psychologist, New York.

Suggested Additional Reading

Chapter One
Jeanette Lauer and Robert Lauer, "Why Marriages Last," *Psychology Today,* (June 1985), pp. 22–26

Chapter Two
Lance Compa, "The Faithful Desperado," *The New York Times Magazine,* (August 4, 1985)

Judith Jobin, "Why Wives Don't Get What They Want," *Woman's Day,* (September 14, 1982) p. 16

Chapter Three
Muriel James and Louis M. Savary, *The Heart of Friendship* (New York: Harper & Row, 1976)

Chapter Four
Carol Gilligan, *In a Different Voice,* (Cambridge, Mass: Harvard University Press 1982)

Walter Menniger, M.D., *Caution: Living May Be Hazardous, Debunking the Happiness Myth* (Kansas City: Sheed, Andrews & McNeel, 1978)

Chapter Five
James Bevan, *The Simon and Schuster Handbook of Anatomy and Physiology* (New York: Simon & Schuster, 1978)

Chapter Six

Deborah Blumenthal, "The Face of Today," Fashions of the Times, *The New York Times Magazine* (August 25, 1985)

Diane Sustendal, "Taking Stock," *New York Times Magazine*, (September 14, 1985)

Chapter Seven

Sandra Harris, *The Double Bed Book* (London: Quartet Books, 1984)

Chapter Eight

Dagmar O'Connor, *How to Make Love to the Same Person for the Rest of Your Life* (New York: Doubleday, 1985)

Chapter Nine

The Lover's Dictionary (London: Hard Lock Limited, 1967)

Nancy Friday, *My Secret Garden* (New York: Pocket Books, 1973)

———, *Forbidden Flowers* (New York: Pocket Books, 1975)

Anaïs Nin, *Delta of Venus* (New York & San Diego: Harcourt Brace Jovanovich, 1977)

Pauline Réage, *Return to the Chateau*. Translated by Sabine D'Estrée (New York: Grove Press, 1971)

Chapter Ten

Travel Section of *The New York Times* (any Sunday)

For further information regarding counseling and/or special workshops the following can be contacted:

American Association of Sex Educators, Counselors and Therapists
2000 N St, N.W.
Suite 110
Washington, D.C. 20036

Academy of Psychologists in Marital Sex and Family Therapy
246 Virginia Avenue
Ft. Lee, New Jersey 07024

American Massage and Therapy Association
P.O. Box 1270
Kingsport, Tennessee 37662

Werner Erhard & Associates
765 California Street
San Francisco, California 94108